SCRIBBLERS AT HOME

SCRIBBLERS AT HOME

Recipes from Lifelong Learners

Scribblers at Home: Recipes from Lifelong Learners

Published by Classical Conversations MultiMedia, Inc.
255 Air Tool Drive
Southern Pines, NC 28387

CLASSICALCONVERSATIONS.COM
CLASSICALCONVERSATIONSBOOKS.COM

Cover design by Classical Conversations.

All Scripture quotations, unless otherwise indicated, are taken from the King James Version of the Bible.

Classical Conversations is excited to partner with military, missionary, and local families on five continents and in more than thirty countries. To find an international community near you, please contact International@ClassicalConversations.com.

May our love of God and His Word turn this world upside-down!

Honoring copyright—it is a matter of integrity!

Printed in the United States of America

ISBN: 978-1-951571-30-6

TABLE OF CONTENTS

Who's Hungry?

Keeping children fed is a full-time, multi-layered project. We must think about nutrition, variety, palate training, and even etiquette. It can't be all chicken nuggets and peanut butter. We want our children to have an appreciation for a wide scope of delicious things. Feeding their minds is very similar. As we help our children taste the world around them, we want to provide a wide variety of beautiful, nutritious, and engaging foods for their growing minds. We want to provide a banquet!

Not just a meal, but a real celebration? A big, splashy, delicious, exuberant celebration? Wouldn't that be fun? And satisfying? The glitter of festive table settings, the aroma of delicious food, the feast for the eyes of perfectly themed decorations—everything coordinated and harmonized? The overall atmosphere of a perfect celebration. We all recognize a good party when we attend one.

But planning a banquet can be a little intimidating. The task can be especially daunting for first-time entertainers. What should the theme be? How will you create the right atmosphere? Who should be invited? What will you serve? Who is going to do the cooking? Where will you find recipes and how-to tips? Where will you get the ingredients?

That's where a good cookbook can help! A good cookbook is a game changer. It provides inspiration, education, motivation, and conversation. When the reader provides dedication, perspiration, and innovation, the partnership is sure to succeed! Cookbooks introduce things that look delicious, and they make recipes doable by giving helpful hints and breaking recipes and meals into easy-to-follow steps. A good cookbook can help with meal planning, choosing new ingredients, learning new skills, putting a dish in context of a meal, thinking about nutrition, enjoying cooking, *and* being adventurous. It takes some of the fear out of cooking by providing solid ideas, tested methods, and fresh perspectives.

Educating your children can be like planning a banquet—a feast you are continually preparing—celebrating the wonder, delight, learning, and warm relationships you want to enjoy as you raise your children. *Scribblers at Home: Recipes from Lifelong Learners* is the inspired yet tried-and-true "cookbook" that helps you prepare for a feast. Let's begin with a question:

What do you want your children to know?

Isn't that the big question when you think about educating your children? Naturally, after you make the decision to educate your children at home, your mind jumps ahead to what to teach them. The first inclination may be to jump in with both feet, devising the plan to engineer the outcome. Most of us believe that the "what" is the next step after the "whether."

But is it?

Suppose we consider other questions first, questions that might guide us more gently toward the celebration we really want to enjoy with our families—a feast of wonder and delight, of entwined lives and joint explorations—a banquet that feeds our families through a lifetime of learning.

Try these questions first:

1. What is your family's purpose?
2. What are your family's priorities?
3. How does education fit into your purpose and priorities?
4. Do you have a family mission statement (a family purpose)?
5. What makes your family unique?
6. How will you identify yourselves?
7. How will you love one another?
8. How will you each give and receive love?
9. What traditions do you have now?
10. What traditions would you like to begin?

These are great conversation starters. Everyone should be involved in the conversation, and you will find many "aha" moments emerging from shared memories and perspectives. As you begin to think about your family mission statement, think deeply about your family's priorities; they will remind you of your purpose when life gets complicated.

Here are some of the questions you can ask as you begin "cooking."

1. What do your little ones need?
2. What do you want to *do* with your little learners?
3. How will you prepare them for lifelong learning?
4. How do you promote wonder, excitement, and constant curiosity?
5. How do you choose your resources? (Do you even need resources?)
6. How can you have continual conversations—even as your children grow and change?
7. How do you keep family time a priority?
8. How do you start your day off right?
9. How can you cultivate teachable moments?

These are the questions that can make your head spin! You may feel like you have to know all about the *how* before you dive into the *what*, but you need the *what* in order to begin.

Be sure to homeschool with a friend. We want to help! Classical Conversations® is dedicated to equipping families, enabling you to educate with confidence and joy. These recipes are designed to prepare you and your family for the most satisfying adventure of your lives and to help you enjoy with assurance the education you live out together.

Take some time to write a family mission statement. A family mission statement is a written statement of what you see as your family's purpose. It can include both how you want your family to grow and what you see as your family's role in the world. If you already have a mission statement, jot it down here; if not, you might use this space to begin brainstorming for your family's mission.

OUR FAMILY MISSION STATEMENT

_____

_____

_____

_____

_____

_____

_____

_____

Here's an example:

Grace and Light Classical Academy exists for the pursuit of spiritual wisdom and academic excellence, developing a family culture of lifelong learning and purposeful adventures that allow us to know God and to make Him known.

—Heatherly Sylvia, mom of the Sylvia family's home school, Grace and Light Classical Academy

The charts preview how Scribblers prepares you for homeschooling older children.

EIGHT PARTS OF SPEECH CHART

Remember, the charts in Scribblers are **parent**-focused; these are intended to redeem your education and to show you where skills-building will take you. Don't skip an activity because the chart is over your child's head; it's for **you**!

The information in each chart provides foundational material in each subject strand. The charts are not always exhaustive, but they give a clear picture of basic knowledge that will continue to grow through study.

Occasionally, you will notice a compass icon on a chart. This icon, and the accompanying text, point you toward the Challenge level (within Classical Conversations) in which your student will continue to practice the skills included on the chart, achieving mastery through repetition.

An **adjective** modifies a noun or pronoun by describing, qualifying, or limiting.
Ask: *What kind? How many? Which? Whose?*

A **noun** names a person, place, thing activity, or idea.
Ask: *Who [verb]? or What [verb]?*

A **verb** is a word that asserts an action, shows a state of being, links two words together, or helps another verb.
Ask: *What is being said about [subject]?*

A **preposition** relates a noun or pronoun to another word.
Memorize the list.

A **pronoun** replaces a noun in order to avoid repetition.
Ask: *Who [verb] or what [verb]? Also, memorize the lists.*

An **interjection** is a word or phrase used as a strong expression of feeling or emotion.
An interjection is set apart from the rest of the sentence by either an exclamation mark, question mark, comma or period. Example: *Oh my!*

An **adverb** modifies a verb, adjective, or another adverb.
Ask: *How? When? Where? Why? How often? How much? To what extent? Under what condition?*

A **conjunction** is a word used to connect words, phrases, or clauses together.
Memorize lists of coordinating conjunctions (FANBOYS), correlative pairs, and subordinating conjunctions (www.asia.wub).

8 PARTS OF SPEECH

adjective (AJ) | noun (N) | verb (V) | pronoun (P) | adverb (AV) | conjunction (C) | interjection (I) | preposition (Pr)

Students study English grammar in Essentials and throughout the Challenge program as they work on becoming better communicators. A firm grasp of grammar prepares students to study all languages more easily. Understanding the structure of language allows students to deconstruct difficult texts as well.

(*Continued from page 11*)

Included in this guide you will find an enchanting selection of poems to enjoy as a family; these can be read to begin each day and might be shared (or memorized) throughout the week. These poems can become the basis of nightly conversations and might easily take the place of evening television.

The recipe and chart section is organized by strand—or course, in our cookbook metaphor. Each strand is introduced by a two-page spread giving some pointers on why and how to approach each strand of learning. Connections between the Scribblers skills introduced and the way these skills are realized in later learning (in the Classical Conversations® Challenge program) are outlined, and you will find tips for how to study and appreciate each strand. Each recipe outlines a child-centered activity with a serving suggestion, prep time advisory, ingredients (supplies) list, and easy-to-follow steps to cook up fun and build new skills. Each parent-centered companion chart offers a core of information—grammar—in a chosen subject. These recipes and charts provide a framework of knowledge for families as they learn the grammar of all strands together. These charts are often a good beginning for Scribblers as well as a helpful reminder for older students who will add to this information as they practice the arts of dialectic and rhetoric throughout their continuing studies. Parents eager to reclaim their own educations will find the charts to be a helpful skeleton on which to build. (See the Example Strand Spread on pages 14–15.)

These recipes are designed to be an encouraging, enlightening, and invigorating suggestion for how to begin a life of exploration with your littlest learners. We know that the days are long and sometimes feel overfull. Remember that building relationships is the important work of home. Our encouragement: **Feast daily** by **praying** together, **playing** together, **reading** together, **exploring** together, and **serving** together. This is the recipe for victorious family living and learning.

"The duty of parents is to sustain a child's inner life with ideas as they sustain his body with food."

—Charlotte Mason, *Parents and Children*, Home Education Series, vol. 2

The help of a team of creative thinkers with playful spirits is gratefully acknowledged.

Stephanie B. Meter, who has always loved stories, and who helped create materials to plant that love in the hearts of families

Kirsty Gilpin, on loan from *The Math Map*, who helped us produce charts that are both accurate and winsome

Denise Moore, a lover of learning and Latin, who created charts that show families how language skills grow

Leslie Hubbard, a wonder-seeker, who created charts that help families explore wonders as they become scientists

Marc Hays, who helped chart the movements of history for students from Scribblers to parents

Cyndi Widman, Karin Carpenter, and Sarah Pederson, who made sure all our i's were dotted and our t's crossed

Sarah McElroy, who applied artistic genius to this beautiful resource, a feast for the eyes

We would also like to thank Pitman Photography and the Classical Conversations communities of Syosset, New York, and Winter Haven, Florida, for their participation in photo shoots that contributed to this publication.

GRAMMAR OF
POETRY

Choosing This Course: **WHY** study poetry

- Poetry opens the world to children! A poem allows us to join a traveling show, become a pirate, or explore a far-off land. Poems encourage us to be fascinated with nature, explore our feelings, and consider "what if . . ." Poems teach us to consider what others may think or feel and to explore situations and feelings that are not our own.

- Reading poetry tickles our ears with words, making language fun or funny in turn. Poetry teaches us the significance of words as we ponder their placements and specific meanings as well as their sounds and the feelings they evoke.

- Reading poetry as a family creates sweet, shared memories and times of imagining together. Families grow closer as they bond over appreciation for a good poem and as they examine the feelings poetry introduces. Reading poetry together can become a restful moment in your day or week, reminding you to savor the moments of being together.

- Poetry contributes to our appreciation for different types of writing. Communicating ideas using rhyme, rhythm, and imagery—within a variety of poetry styles—opens a new avenue for sharing thoughts and experiences.

Basic Ingredients: **WHAT** should be included

Families will enjoy reading poetry most when a variety of poetry types are sampled. In Scribblers, families will find riddles, chain tales, and nursery rhymes; there are poems that tell stories, poems that celebrate families, and poems that recall the beauty of nature. Devour them all, knowing that all types have their place in developing the young reader's palate. Look for:

- **Riddles** – questions that require creative thinking to arrive at the solution, which sometimes involve a pun or other play on words

- **Chain tales** – a cumulative story in which new pieces are added and previous pieces are repeated in order to aid memory

- **Storytelling or narrative poems** – poems that tell a story

- **Family culture poetry** – poems that feature everyday life or family relationships

- **Nursery rhymes** – short, simple poems designed for children

- **Nature poems** – poems that celebrate the beauty of nature

- **Character poems** – poems (written in third or first person) that are about a character, either real or fictional

Learning to Cook: **HOW** to become poets

- **Reading** poetry aloud can be a delight for the senses and a delightful shared experience for families with all ages. Many families find a morning reading time to be a gentle way to begin the day; poetry certainly has its place there. Simply enjoying the sounds of the words leads to the exploration of phonics and why words rhyme, and it can introduce grand imaginative conversations.

- Oftentimes, poems are the first pieces of memory work a child masters; the lilting words broken into manageable chunks make easy memory pegs for our littlest learners. **Memorizing** poems together as a family creates common connections with literature and with the process of memorizing.

- **Reciting** poems is an easy way to begin teaching children the basics of how to present to others. Reciting memorized poems to grandparents, neighbors, or friends allows children to share something they like and to share an accomplishment.

- Another way to enjoy poetry with your children is **copying** and **illustrating** the poem you are reading or memorizing. Copywork is excellent training for children's eyes and hands as they learn to read and write, and it is an easy way to practice penmanship. Illustrating poems allows children to connect with the poem in another way as they decide what images, colors, shapes, and media to use.

The Challenge of Poetry: **WHEN** you are ready for more

- Training the ears to appreciate poetry doesn't end with Scribblers. From the Psalms and Shakespeare's sonnets to the epic poetry of Homer's *The Iliad* and *The Odyssey*, students will study various forms of poetry, learning to appreciate poetic language and the impact of different forms of poetry.

- Students will encounter haiku, shape poems, acrostics, senryu, and narrative poems, and they will spend time in community reading, discussing, memorizing, writing, and presenting these and other forms of poetic expression.

	SCRIBBLERS/FOUNDATIONS		FOUNDATIONS/ESSENTIALS		CHALLENGE
☐	five senses	☐	five senses	☐	five senses
☐	notebook	☐	notebook	☐	notebook
☐	crayons/pencils	☐	pencils/highlighters	☐	pencils/highlighters
☐	Bible	☐	syllabication rules	☐	thesaurus
☐	poetry anthologies	☐	*The Synonym Finder*	☐	*The Synonym Finder*
☐	nursery rhyme books	☐	Bible	☐	guide to poetic forms
☐	hymnals	☐	poetry anthologies, hymnals	☐	list of rhetorical devices
☐		☐	rhyming dictionary	☐	Bible
☐		☐		☐	poetry anthologies, hymnals
☐		☐		☐	rhyming dictionary

TOOLS FOR EVERY AGE

POETRY

I CAUGHT A FISH ALIVE

One, two, three, four, five,
I caught a fish alive;
Six, seven, eight, nine, ten,
I have let it go again.
Why did you let it go?
Because it bit my finger so.
Which finger did it bite?
The little one upon the right.

AUTHOR UNKNOWN

Poem from *The Happy Nursery Rhyme Book* compiled by Christopher Wood (New York: T. Y. Crowell Co., 1914).

Image: "Fisherman." Etching and engraving by Claude Augustin Duflos le Jeune from Metropolitan Museum of Art (c. 1753).

POETRY

MR. NOBODY

I know a funny little man,
As quiet as a mouse,
Who does the mischief that is done
In everybody's house!
There's no one ever sees his face,
And yet we all agree
That every plate we break was cracked
By Mr. Nobody.

'Tis he who always tears our books,
Who leaves the door ajar,
He pulls the buttons from our shirts,
And scatters pins afar;
That squeaking door will always squeak,
For prithee, don't you see,
We leave the oiling to be done
By Mr. Nobody.

He puts damp wood upon the fire
That kettles cannot boil;
His are the feet that bring in mud,
And all the carpets soil.
The papers always are mislaid;
Who had them last, but he?
There's no one tosses them about
But Mr. Nobody.

The finger marks upon the door
By none of us are made;
We never leave the blinds unclosed,
To let the curtains fade.
The ink we never spill; the boots
That lying round you see
Are not our boots,—they all belong
To Mr. Nobody.

AUTHOR UNKNOWN

Poem from *Willson's Intermediate Fifth Reader* by Marcius Willson (New York: Harper & Brothers, 1870).

Image: "A tiny man with funny hair sitting in a top hat reading the newspaper." Illustration from *Marjorie and Her Papa, How They Wrote a Story and Made Pictures for It* by Robert Howe Fletcher (New York: The Century Co., 1904).

POETRY

THE PASTURE

I'm going out to clean the pasture spring;
I'll only stop to rake the leaves away
(And wait to watch the water clear, I may):
I sha'n't be gone long.—You come too.

I'm going out to fetch the little calf
That's standing by the mother. It's so young,
It totters when she licks it with her tongue.
I sha'n't be gone long.—You come too.

—ROBERT FROST
(1874–1963)

Poem from *Selected Poems* by Robert Frost (New York: Henry Holt & Co., 1923).

Image: "Cows in the Meadow." Painting by Girard Bilders (c. 1860–1865).

POETRY

LADYBUG

Ladybug, ladybug,
    Fly away, do;

Fly to the mountain,
    And feed upon dew.

Feed upon dew,
    And sleep on a rug,

And then run away
    Like a good little bug.

AUTHOR UNKNOWN

Poem from *The Latch Key of My Bookhouse* edited by Olive Beaupré Miller (Chicago: Bookhouse for Children, 1921).

Image: Eyed Lady-Bird, *Coccinella ocellata. The Encyclopedia Britannica, New Werner Edition* (New York: The Werner Co., 1893).

POETRY

THE DOVE

Out of the sunshine and out of the heat,
Out of the dust of the grimy street,
A song fluttered down in the form of a dove,
And it bore me a message, the one word—Love!

Ah, I was toiling, and oh, I was sad:
I had forgotten the way to be glad.
Now, smiles for my sadness and for my toil, rest
Since the dove fluttered down to its home in my breast!

—PAUL LAURENCE DUNBAR
(1872–1906)

Poem from *The Complete Poems of Paul Laurence Dunbar* by Paul Laurence Dunbar (New York: Dodd, Mead & Co., 1913).

Image: "Dove returns with olive branch." Etching and engraving by Bernard Picart (c. 1720).

RIDDLES

Formed long ago, yet made today,
Employed while others sleep;
What few would like to give away,
Nor any wish to keep.

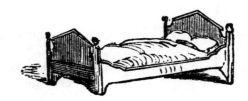

I went to the wood and got it;
I sat me down and looked at it;
The more I looked at it the less I liked it;
And I brought it home because I couldn't help it.

Thomas a Tattamus took two *T*'s,
To tie two tups* to two tall trees,
To frighten the terrible Thomas a Tattamus!
Tell me how many *T*'s there are in all that.

AUTHORS UNKNOWN

*A tup is an adult male sheep.

Answers: 1. A bed. 2. A thorn. 3. Two *T*'s in "that."

Poems from "Riddles and Paradoxes" in *The Nursery Rhyme Book* edited by Andrew Lang (London: Frederick Warne & Co., 1897).

Images (top to bottom): 1. "An illustration of a bed." Illustration from *Our Young Folks: An Illustrated Magazine for Boys and Girls* (Boston, MA: Ticknor and Fields, 1866). 2. "Aculeus.—A prickle or sharp point, from the bark." Illustration by John B. Newman from *Illustrated Botany* (New York: Fowler & Wells, 1850). 3. "This letter *T* is a rustic letter design, typically used by gardeners or florists for its branch-like style." Illustration by F. Maire from *Modern Painter's Cyclopedia* (Chicago, IL: Frederick J. Drake & Co., 1918).

POETRY

APRIL RAIN SONG

Let the rain kiss you.
Let the rain beat upon your heat with silver liquid drops.
Let the rain sing you a lullaby.

The rain makes still pools on the sidewalk.
The rain makes running pools in the gutter.
The rain plays a little sleep-song on our roof at night—

And I love the rain.

—LANGSTON HUGHES
(1902–1967)

Poem from *The Brownies Book*, W. E. B. Du Bois, contributor (New York: DuBois and Dill, 1920).

Image: "Girl walking in rain with doll and umbrella." Illustration from *Boys' and Girls' Bookshelf*, volume 4 (New York: The University Society, 1920).

ONE, TWO, BUCKLE MY SHOE

One, two, buckle my shoe;

Three, four, shut the door;

Five, six, pick up sticks;

Seven, eight, lay them straight;

Nine, ten, a good fat hen;

Eleven, twelve, who will delve?

Thirteen, fourteen, maid's a-courting;

Fifteen, sixteen, maids a-kissing;

Seventeen, eighteen, maids a-waiting;

Nineteen, twenty, my stomach's empty.

AUTHOR UNKNOWN

Poem and illustration ("One, Two, Buckle My Shoe") from *Mother Goose's Nursery Rhymes: A Collection of Alphabets, Rhymes, Tales, and Jingles* illustrated by Walter Crane et al. (New York: McLoughlin Brothers, 1899).

POETRY

YOUNG NIGHT THOUGHT

All night long and every night,
When my mamma puts out the light,
I see the people marching by,
As plain as day, before my eye.

Armies and emperors and kings,
All carrying different kinds of things,
And marching in so grand a way,
You never saw the like by day.

So fine a show was never seen,
At the great circus on the green;
For every kind of beast and man
Is marching in that caravan.

At first they move a little slow
But still the faster on they go,
And still beside them close I keep
Until we reach the town of Sleep.

—ROBERT LOUIS STEVENSON
(1850–1894)

Poem from *A Child's Garden of Verses* by Robert Louis Stevenson (New York: Charles Scribner's Sons, 1909).

Image: "Young Night Thought." Illustration by Florence Edith Storer from *A Child's Garden of Verses* by Robert Louis Stevenson (New York: Charles Scribner's Sons, 1909).

DICTATION CHART

Although they are related skills, copywork and dictation are actually different activities. Both are an important part of language instruction for young students. Copywork emphasizes visual attention. If a parent creates a sentence on a paper or a whiteboard and asks the student to copy it, the student must visually attend to the capitals, correct spelling, spacing between words, and punctuation marks. Dictation emphasizes aural attention. The student must listen to each word as the parent states it, create a mental image of that word, and then reproduce the word on the paper. Then, students must visually attend to the sentence and make sure they have included proper spelling and punctuation. Both visual and aural attention are important skills that lead to reading success and proficiency.

FIVE PARTS OF A COMPLETE SENTENCE	
1	**Subject.** Every sentence has a subject. It answers the question: *Who or what is this sentence about?*
2	**Predicate.** Every sentence has a predicate, which can be a single verb or many words. The predicate answers the question: *What is being said about the subject?*
3	**Capital letter.** Every sentence begins with a capital letter.
4	**End mark.** Every sentence ends with an end mark. The choices are period (.), exclamation mark (!), or question mark (?).
5	**Complete sense.** The sentence must express a complete thought. An example is: **Bob runs.** This is a complete sentence. An example of a fragment is: **on the shelf.** This is not a sentence because it does not express a complete thought.

TIPS FOR DICTATING SENTENCES TO CHILDREN	
1	**Speak slowly** enough for the child to keep up.
2	**Enunciate the words** clearly so that the child can practice spelling rules.
3	**Repeat the sentence** several times.
4	**Exaggerate voice inflection** so that it is clear when the student needs an exclamation mark or a question mark.
5	**Start small.** Dictate short sentences until it is easy for the student, and then increase the length.
6	**Practice spelling rules.** Dictate sentences that include spelling words the child is currently practicing or words that the child commonly misspells.
7	**Mix it up.** Dictate sentences from a book you have been reading, from Foundations memory work, or from Scripture. Make it fun!
8	**Check their work.** Look over sentences carefully with your students to make sure they have used correct punctuation and spelling (see Sentence Mechanics Chart and Spelling Rules Chart).

"Drawing an accurate picture with words takes time, just like painting a portrait. Seeing and replicating details carefully make it possible to produce art of good quality. You want your children to be word craftsmen."
—Leigh Bortins, *The Core* (115)

SERVING SUGGESTION: When you're in a storytelling mood

PREP TIME: 5 minutes

INGREDIENTS: Sentence Mechanics Chart (right), *Old World Echoes*, perhaps some drawing materials

STEPS: Attending to the details of mechanics is a core habit; storytelling can make that habit fun!

1. Read the poem "The Owl and the Pussycat" and talk about how punctuation gives us "signals" about the story. Your littlest learners may also enjoy drawing a picture of what they hear. You may choose another poem if you like.

2. Have your young readers look at the poem to see how the lines (called "stanzas") are grouped together.

3. Discuss punctuation marks and what they mean; demonstrate some of these marks on paper or whiteboard.

4. Read the poem again, asking your child to point out the punctuation marks—a punctuation scavenger hunt!

5. You might ask your child to make note of certain punctuation marks routinely until they become familiar: semi-colon Saturdays, question mark Mondays, etc.

6. Next, notice the capital letters at the beginning of each line. Have your child think about whether each capital marks the beginning of a sentence.

7. Find a sentence in the poem and model reading it with different punctuation; read with emphasis or excitement, as though the punctuation were an exclamation mark. Show how a question mark changes the inflection of your voice.

YIELD: Children who are attuned to attending well and know that "playing" with words and punctuation is rewarding and enjoyable

TIPS AND HINTS

Paying attention to details is how we get better at the nuances of almost everything. Before your children master the mechanics of writing or grammar, they need to notice some of those mechanics. As you point out the punctuation in the stories and poems you read, you help your children gather clues about how to read or tell a story and what a difference little details can make.

SENTENCE MECHANICS CHART

Capitalize the first letter of every sentence.	*Do this every time.*
Use the appropriate **end mark** for the purpose of the sentence, such as period (.), exclamation mark (!), or question mark (?).	*Do you understand?*
Capitalize *I* when used as a word.	*He and I are happy.*
Capitalize all **proper nouns**.	*I love Jesus.*
Most **possessive nouns** end with either -'s if singular, or -s' if plural. Possessive pronouns, such as *yours, theirs, ours,* etc., do not require an apostrophe.	*Run! It is the monster that eats the boys' lunches when the girl's monkey opens its cage!*
Abbreviations end with a period except for abbreviated state names and abbreviated metric units of measure.	*Mr. Jones lived in Troy, NC, from Jan. through Mar.* *The ruler is 30 cm long.*
Use commas to **separate items** in a series.	*The big, fat, brown hog ate the swill, the slops, and the corn husks.*
Use a comma or commas to surround **appositives** and **nouns of direct address**.	*I, Jill Pill, gave him, my brother, a dollar bill.* *Nolan, come outside to play!*
Use a comma before the conjunction in a **compound sentence**.	*Jack and Jill are nice, but I am nicer.*
If two **independent clauses** joined by a conjunction are short and closely related in thought, the comma may be omitted.	*I will walk and he will run.*
Use a comma or commas to separate the subordinate clause from the independent clause in a **complex sentence** unless the subordinate clause follows the independent clause.	*When we play, we have fun.* *We, who have fun, play.* *We have fun when we play.*
Use **quotation marks** before and after a speaker's exact words.	*"We live!" shouted the man.* *The man shouted, "We live!" (Note the use of the comma.)*
Use **dashes** to indicate an abrupt thought, to set off parenthetical information, or before an author's name when it follows a direct quote.	*He gave the right to become children of God—not of natural descent.*
Use a **hyphen** (-) (a) to link compound adjectives, (b) to express numbers 21–99 in words, also fractions, (c) to divide words at the end of a line, or (d) to replace a connecting word, in particular between figures (use an **en dash** [–] when typing).	*The soft-spoken*[a] *teacher had forty-two*[b] *hundred former students attend her retirement din-ner,*[c] *which was from 2–4 p.m.*[d]
A semicolon (;) may be used to **replace a conjunction** in a compound sentence.	*We love Jesus; they adore Jesus.*
Use a **colon** (:) (a) to introduce a list or question, (b) between hours/minutes/seconds in time, or (c) between chapter and verse or volume and page numbers in references or footnotes.	*The following verses must be memorized by 3:00*[b]*:*[a] *Genesis 2:5,*[c] *Philippians 4:8,*[c] *and 1 Corinthians 10:13.*[c]
Use **parentheses** (()) (a) to enclose information not pertinent to thought, (b) to enclose numbered/lettered items in a sentence, or (c) to enclose a reference in a sentence.	*Harriet Tubman (1820–1913)*[a] *led the Underground Railroad (Scholastic American History Homework pp. 54–55)*[c]*. She also worked for the Union during the Civil War as a (a) cook, (b) spy, and (c)*[b] *nurse.*

PHONICS

SERVING SUGGESTION: The car, house, park, playground, or doctor's office

PREP TIME: 5 minutes

INGREDIENTS: Eight Parts of Speech Chart (at right)—noun section

STEPS: Patterning how to learn in an engaging way helps your child for a lifetime.

1. Chant the definition of a noun three times with your child.
2. Look around your area and name **people**, **places**, and **things**.
3. Give an example of an **activity**, such as running, and have your child name other activities.
4. Give an example of an **idea**, such as the fruits of the Spirit (love, joy, peace, patience, kindness, goodness, gentleness, self-control). Or ask your child to name feelings.
5. Gather a few stuffed animals or animal figurines and invent alternative names for them based on what your children observe about them. For example, you might rename a giraffe "Mr. Long Neck."

Repeat in three other locations this week.

YIELD: A child who is familiar with grammar categories and has a basic understanding of nouns

TIPS AND HINTS

Tell your child how you chose his name. Read about people whose names were changed: Jacob (Genesis 32), Benjamin (Genesis 35), and Simon Peter (Matthew 16). Memorize Luke 10:20.

EIGHT PARTS OF SPEECH CHART

An **adjective** *modifies a noun or pronoun by describing, qualifying, or limiting.*

Ask: *What kind? How many? Which? Whose?*

A **noun** *names a person, place, thing activity, or idea.*

Ask: *Who [verb]? or What [verb]?*

A **verb** *is a word that asserts an action, shows a state of being, links two words together, or helps another verb.*

Ask: *What is being said about [subject]?*

A **preposition** *relates a noun or pronoun to another word.*

Memorize the list.

An **interjection** *is a word or phrase used as a strong expression of feeling or emotion.*

An interjection is set apart from the rest of the sentence by either an exclamation mark, question mark, comma or period. Example: *Oh my!*

A **pronoun** *replaces a noun in order to avoid repetition.*

Ask: *Who [verb] or what [verb]?* Also, memorize the lists.

An **adverb** *modifies a verb, adjective, or another adverb.*

Ask: *How? When? Where? Why? How often? How much? To what extent? Under what condition?*

A **conjunction** *is a word used to connect words, phrases, or clauses together.*

Memorize lists of coordinating conjunctions (FANBOYS), correlative pairs, and subordinating conjunctions (www.asia.wub).

8 PARTS OF SPEECH

- adjective (AJ)
- noun (N)
- verb (V)
- preposition (Pr)
- pronoun (P)
- interjection (I)
- adverb (AV)
- conjunction (C)

Students study English grammar in Essentials and throughout the Challenge program as they work on becoming better communicators. A firm grasp of grammar prepares students to study all languages more easily. Understanding the structure of language allows students to deconstruct difficult texts as well.

QUESTION CONFIRMATION CHART

1 Identify **INDEPENDENT** and **SUBORDINATE** clauses.

2 **WHO** or **WHAT** is the sentence about? (This identifies the subject.)

3 **WHAT** is being said about the subject? (This identifies the verb.)

ALL sentences must contain a subject and a predicate.

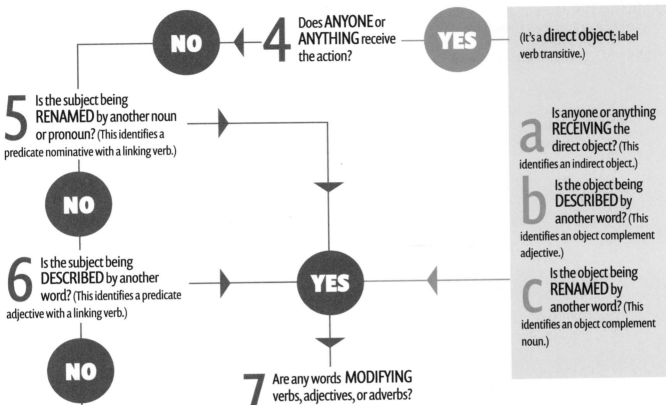

NO

4 Does **ANYONE** or **ANYTHING** receive the action?

YES (It's a **direct object**; label verb transitive.)

a Is anyone or anything **RECEIVING** the direct object? (This identifies an indirect object.)

b Is the object being **DESCRIBED** by another word? (This identifies an object complement adjective.)

c Is the object being **RENAMED** by another word? (This identifies an object complement noun.)

5 Is the subject being **RENAMED** by another noun or pronoun? (This identifies a predicate nominative with a linking verb.)

NO

6 Is the subject being **DESCRIBED** by another word? (This identifies a predicate adjective with a linking verb.)

NO

Label the verb intransitive.

YES

7 Are any words **MODIFYING** verbs, adjectives, or adverbs? (This identifies adverbs.)

8 Are any words **MODIFYING** nouns or pronouns? (This identifies adjectives.)

9 Are there any **PREPOSITIONAL PHRASES**? (Label the preposition, its noun object, and any modifiers. Is it adjectival or adverbial? Identify the word that it modifies.)

10 Are there any **CONJUNCTIONS**? (Does it join a compound subject, a compound predicate, a compound sentence, or something else?)

11 Are there any **INTERJECTIONS**?

IDENTIFY the sentence structure, purpose, and pattern.

CONGRATULATIONS! YOU HAVE A SENTENCE!

We want to help students achieve mastery over what they read and what they write. Classical Conversations students will learn English from the roots up through intensive grammar studies in Essentials and will employ their knowledge to craft better sentences as they communicate in papers, presentations, and conversations.

PHONICS

SERVING SUGGESTION: Outside porch, patio, or deck

PREP TIME: 10 minutes

INGREDIENTS: Diagramming Chart (at right), painter's tape, action cards (see below), cards with family members' names, 2–3 bananas

STEPS:
1. Using painter's tape, secure tape to floor to make a six-foot horizontal line.
2. Tape two vertical lines dividing the horizontal line evenly at two-foot intervals. Each vertical line should be perpendicular to the horizontal line. The first vertical line should cross the horizontal line, and the second vertical line should come to rest on the horizontal line. Your floor diagram should have three two-foot divisions that allow space for the subject of the sentence, the verb, and the direct object.

Subject	Verb-transitive	Direct Object
S	Vt	DO
Cats	stalk	mice

3. Make action cards using these verbs: *slaps, throws, hides, praises, juggles, cuddles, squeezes, kisses, stomps, serenades.* If your family enjoys this game, you can add more verbs.
4. Make cards with each family member's name.
5. Divide the cards into two piles: names and verbs.
6. Place the bananas in the last section of your taped sentence diagram model. This is the direct object of your sentence.
7. Draw one card from each pile. The chosen family member stands in the subject section (the first section) and places the verb card in the verb section (the middle section).
8. The chosen player dramatically acts out the sentence with the banana.
9. Take a few silly pictures!

YIELD: Children with increased familiarity and comfort with the parts of a sentence

TIPS AND HINTS

What does self-confidence have to do with diagramming a sentence? (No, this is not a set up for a joke.) Think about it. How many times have you written a sentence and wondered if it was a fragment or a run-on sentence? Writing reflects who we are, and most of us feel a lack of confidence when we put pen to paper. Realizing that our language is logically structured gives us a way to evaluate writing. One of the best ways to gain this understanding is to visually evaluate how the words in a sentence fit together through diagramming. When we take a sentence apart and categorize each word by function, we are able to recognize any gaps or mistakes. As we grow more familiar with the grammatical structure of sentences, we gain confidence in our writing. Then, as parents, we are able to pass this confidence on to our children.

DIAGRAMMING CHART

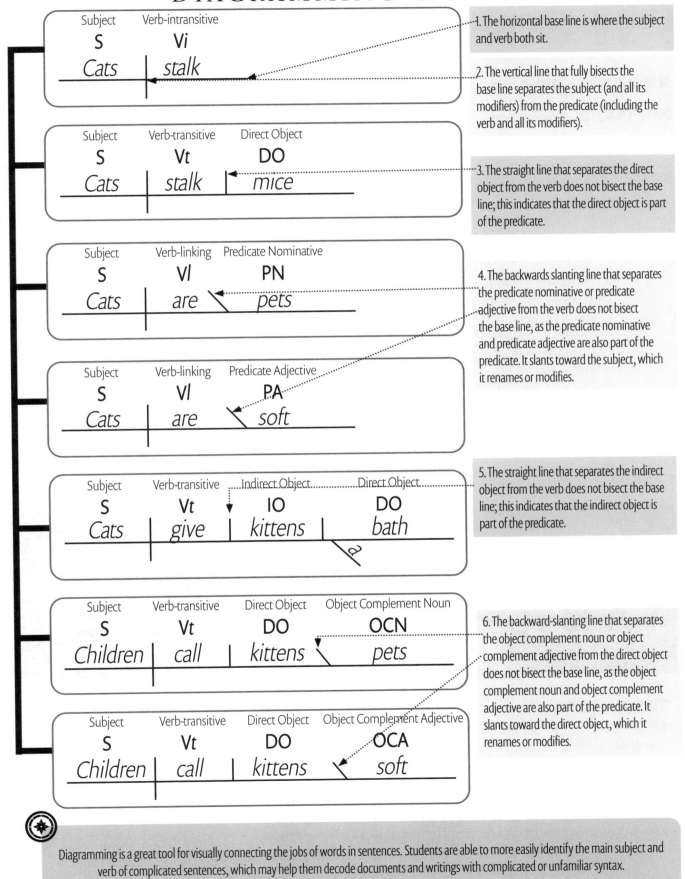

Subject	Verb-intransitive
S	Vi
Cats	stalk

1. The horizontal base line is where the subject and verb both sit.

2. The vertical line that fully bisects the base line separates the subject (and all its modifiers) from the predicate (including the verb and all its modifiers).

Subject	Verb-transitive	Direct Object
S	Vt	DO
Cats	stalk	mice

3. The straight line that separates the direct object from the verb does not bisect the base line; this indicates that the direct object is part of the predicate.

Subject	Verb-linking	Predicate Nominative
S	Vl	PN
Cats	are	pets

4. The backwards slanting line that separates the predicate nominative or predicate adjective from the verb does not bisect the base line, as the predicate nominative and predicate adjective are also part of the predicate. It slants toward the subject, which it renames or modifies.

Subject	Verb-linking	Predicate Adjective
S	Vl	PA
Cats	are	soft

Subject	Verb-transitive	Indirect Object	Direct Object
S	Vt	IO	DO
Cats	give	kittens	bath

5. The straight line that separates the indirect object from the verb does not bisect the base line; this indicates that the indirect object is part of the predicate.

Subject	Verb-transitive	Direct Object	Object Complement Noun
S	Vt	DO	OCN
Children	call	kittens	pets

6. The backward-slanting line that separates the object complement noun or object complement adjective from the direct object does not bisect the base line, as the object complement noun and object complement adjective are also part of the predicate. It slants toward the direct object, which it renames or modifies.

Subject	Verb-transitive	Direct Object	Object Complement Adjective
S	Vt	DO	OCA
Children	call	kittens	soft

Diagramming is a great tool for visually connecting the jobs of words in sentences. Students are able to more easily identify the main subject and verb of complicated sentences, which may help them decode documents and writings with complicated or unfamiliar syntax.

PHONICS

SERVING SUGGESTION: At the library

PREP TIME: 10–15 minutes

INGREDIENTS: Favorite picture books, tracing paper, index cards, pencils, tape (painter's tape works best)

STEPS:
1. Visit your local library and have everyone choose a favorite picture book.
2. Find the names of the author, illustrator, and publisher. Make a note of the copyright date. Briefly discuss each person's job.
3. Record this information for each book on an index card.
4. Ask each person to look through his book and pick out a favorite illustration and quote.
5. Using tracing paper, trace the illustration and write out the favorite quote on an index card.
6. At home, place the tracings in one stack, the quotes in another, and the source cards in another. Take turns matching the source information with the quote and tracing. Show your picture and read your quote. Talk about what you liked about this author's work.
7. Try making up a new song to help you remember who does what in creating a book. Use the tune "The Farmer in the Dell," and sing a verse for each job: "The author writes the book, the author writes the book. Hi-ho the derry-o, the author writes the book." Then, the illustrator draws the pictures, the editor fixes the words, and the publisher makes the book.
8. As an extension, find the author and illustrator online. Many authors and illustrators have fan clubs, which include contact information. Take a few minutes to write a short thank-you note, thanking them for their talented writing and illustrating.

YIELD: An understanding of the importance of appreciating and honoring an author's or illustrator's work

TIPS AND HINTS

Paying attention to details like proofreading and citing sources is an act of integrity and humility. It's a way of considering your audience's needs and saying "thank you" for your sources' diligent labor. As parents, we can start this practice with our learners early by simply recognizing acts of service others do. "Thank you" are some of the kindest and most honest words you can teach your children to speak! In 1 Thessalonians 5, Paul says there are three things we are told that are the will of God in Christ Jesus. One of them is "to give thanks in everything." Start early modeling of thankfulness and encourage your children to recognize others' work on their behalf.

> "Rejoice evermore. Pray without ceasing. In every thing give thanks: for this is the will of God in Christ Jesus concerning you." (1 Thessalonians 5:16–18)

PROOFREADING CHART

Ten Tips for Proofreading Effectively

1. **Give it a rest.** If time allows, set your text aside for a few hours (or days) after you've finished composing, and then proofread it with fresh eyes.

2. **Look for one type of problem at a time.** Read through your text several times, concentrating first on sentence structures, then word choice, then spelling, then punctuation, etc.

3. **Double-check facts, figures, and proper names.** In addition to reviewing for correct spelling and usage, make sure that all of the information is accurate.

4. **Review a hard copy.** Print out your text and review it line by line; rereading your work in a different format may help you catch errors that you previously missed.

5. **Read your text aloud.** Or better yet, ask a friend to read it aloud. You may hear a problem you haven't been able to see.

6. **Use a spellchecker.** The spellchecker can help you catch repeated words, reversed letters, and many other common errors—but it's certainly not goof-proof.

7. **Trust your dictionary.** Your spellchecker can tell you only if a word is a word, not if it's the right word. If the spelling of a word causes you to hesitate for even a second, reach for your dictionary.

8. **Read your text backward.** Another way to catch spelling errors is to read backward, from right to left, starting with the last word in your text. Doing this will help you focus on individual words rather than sentences.

9. **Create your own proofreading checklist.** Keep a list of the types of mistakes you commonly make, and then refer to that list each time you proofread.

10. **Ask for help.** Invite someone else to proofread your text after you have reviewed it. A new set of eyes may immediately spot errors that you've overlooked.

Proofreading Checklist

STAGE 1: CONTENT REVIEW

Sense, Clarity, and Flow
- ☐ Text makes sense and flows well; nothing is missing and nothing is repeated.
- ☐ Wording is clear and appropriate for intended audience.
- ☐ Sentences use clear subjects and vivid verbs.

Spelling and Capitalization
- ☐ Spelling and usage of common words are correct.
- ☐ Spelling and capitalization of proper names and special terms are consistent.

Grammar
- ☐ Subjects and verbs agree.
- ☐ Verbs are in correct tense.
- ☐ Pronouns agree with their referents and are in correct case.
- ☐ Modifiers are placed correctly to keep meanings clear.

Punctuation
- ☐ There is no missing, duplicated, or misplaced punctuation.
- ☐ Apostrophes are used only for possessives and contractions.
- ☐ Ellipsis points (…) are used to indicate an omission from a quoted passage.
- ☐ A comma, without connecting conjunction, is not used to separate complete sentences (use stronger punctuation).
- ☐ There are opening and closing parentheses, brackets, and quotation marks.
- ☐ Double and single quotation marks are used correctly.
- ☐ Periods and commas are inside quotation marks; semicolons and colons are outside; other punctuation is inside or outside as appropriate to content.

Research
- ☐ Quotations are cited correctly. Bibliography lists sources correctly.

STAGE 2: FORMATTING REVIEW

Headers and Footers
- ☐ Page numbering is consecutive and appears on all pages in the correct place.
- ☐ Overall layout is pleasing and presents content effectively.

Spacing
- ☐ Margins on all sides are standard and appropriate.
- ☐ Lines of text are spaced appropriately and consistently (e.g., double-spaced).

Fonts and Symbols
- ☐ Italic, bold, and other special fonts are used consistently.
- ☐ One font and size is used consistently (e.g., Times New Roman, 10 pt.).

Parents, you will begin as your child's "proofreader," but you will be working your way out of a job as you teach your student these tips! Students can learn to proof as they learn to write, and Challenge students will need to learn how to cite their sources as they research for papers, presentations, and debates.

READ-ALOUD TIP CHART

Choose an interesting story, or let children choose. (See resource lists in the appendix.)

Find a comfy spot. (Find a rug, the sofa, a hammock, a picnic blanket, or the porch swing.)

Occupy their hands. (Try plastic building blocks, coloring, crafts, or pattern blocks.)

Vary your expression. (Make up voices; alter your volume; use hand gestures.)

Watch your pace. (Read slowly enough for children to process without losing interest.)

Stop to ask questions. (Ask children what is happening or what they think will happen next.)

Check the pulse. (Watch for signs that they have reached their listening capacity.)

Later, ask them to tell back the story. (This is narration.)

Milk the cow. (Read every day!)

Press on. (Read to the children even into their adult years; have older children read aloud too.)

LITERATURE

SERVING SUGGESTION: The porch swing, a chair by the fire, a blanket in the park, or a log in the woods

PREP TIME: 5 minutes

INGREDIENTS: *Old World Echoes*, some fertile imagination

STEPS:

1. Read "Rumpelstiltskin" from *Old World Echoes*. Today you will work on the skills of narration and storytelling as you enjoy some stories with your children. If you don't own this book, choose another tale, or find another version of "Rumpelstiltskin."

2. After reading the story, try to retell the story by taking very short turns. Perhaps you will begin with "Once upon a time in the woods lived a miller with a beautiful daughter. . . .", then invite the next child to add the next bit of the story. Continue to build the story, one sentence at a time, until the tale is told. This retelling will teach the how-tos of "chain stories," an approachable way to begin writing stories of your own and a great way to build family spirit.

3. Chain stories are tales created by multiple storytellers in which the action or dialogue repeats and builds up in some way as the tale progresses. Chain stories are loads of fun and allow your littles to create without feeling the pressure to make up a whole story at once. You can practice this skill in any place at all with no supplies needed. Simply designate someone to begin with "Once upon a time . . ." or "It was a dark and stormy night. . . ." or any opening line at all. Each participant adds a line (or a few lines) in turn, choosing how the story will continue. Littlest learners may need more guidance at first, or you might start them off with a couple of sentences. Older storytellers might enjoy finishing a phrase instead of a sentence!

4. This week, spend some time practicing chain tales. You can even write a new one of your own! If you have mostly littles, work on retelling a read-aloud story one line at a time.

YIELD: Children who can recognize, appreciate, and emulate good writing

TIPS AND HINTS

Our littles catch the idea of how to tell a story well when we read them well-told tales. We gently hone their abilities as we lead them to narrate stories we've shared. Then we encourage them to create stories a little at a time, with help from more practiced storytellers. This is a very classical way to teach: model a behavior or activity, work on a model with them, and let them try it solo (or sort-of solo). The classical model is a time-tested method with clear results. The greatest teacher of all time, Jesus, taught His disciples in much the same way! He modeled meeting the needs of people He saw, He allowed the disciples to work with Him as He met needs, and He empowered the disciples to meet the needs of the people they ministered to after Jesus himself was gone. Consider the stories of Jesus healing the blind man in John 9:1–11, Jesus feeding the five thousand in John 6:1–13, and Peter and John healing the crippled beggar in Acts 3:1–10.

TYPES OF PROSE CHART

There are three main kinds of literature: prose, poetry, and drama. Prose is usually defined in contrast to poetry: Prose writing or speech does not have a regular meter like poetry. Prose is organized writing or speech that is consciously assembled by the author or speaker and organized into a flow. It is also usually characterized by a particular style, which might be an author's word choice or the use of rhetorical devices (see Rhetorical Devices Chart). The word "prose" comes from the Latin *proversus*, which carries the sense of "straightforward" to contrast prose from poetry.

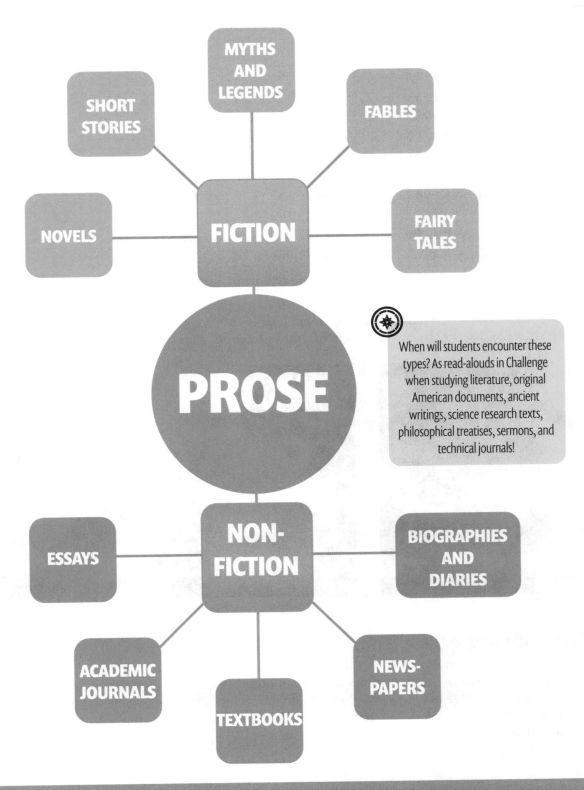

When will students encounter these types? As read-alouds in Challenge when studying literature, original American documents, ancient writings, science research texts, philosophical treatises, sermons, and technical journals!

LITERATURE

SERVING SUGGESTION: Whenever you and your children want to bring a story to life

PREP TIME: 5 minutes

INGREDIENTS: Parts of a Drama Chart (at right), *Old World Echoes*, prop- or costume-making materials

STEPS:
1. Read the story "The Frog Prince" from *Old World Echoes*, and explore how the story might be presented as a drama. You could also use another story that your child knows well.

2. Discuss the characters by asking questions: *What do they look like? What do they wear? What are their attitudes?* Consider how those characteristics might manifest themselves in clothing, accessories, facial expressions, or tone of voice.

3. Discuss the plot by asking more questions: *What does the princess do first? When does she meet the frog? What does the frog ask? What happens next?* Make a list of the main actions, in order.

4. Depending on the ages and abilities of your children, create a play that will retell the story. You may write the story down or not, make costumes or not, perform for an audience or not!

5. Ponder this: *Are there lessons to be learned from the princess's actions? From the frog's? From the king's?* Do your children want to imitate any of the characters? Why or why not?

YIELD: A deeper understanding of narrative skills by engaging in a different way of telling a story. Deconstructing a story in order to put it together in another form also gives us the opportunity to expose the "lessons" in character development a story might offer; "lessons" may be more winsome when children discover them on their own as they look beneath the surface to do a project.

TIPS AND HINTS

Do we ever judge someone by the way they present themselves—their clothing, their facial expressions, or their words? Do we make assumptions about others based on expectations from past experiences? How does God judge us? How should we evaluate one another? Paul offers us some insight in Galatians 2:6 and following. As many parents through the years have maintained, "Actions speak louder than words."

PARTS OF A DRAMA CHART

Drama is one of the three genres of literature along with prose and poetry (refer to Prose and Poetry charts). The Greek philosopher Aristotle was the first to define drama as he examined Greek tragedies and comedies. Drama is a story told by actors who represent the characters. The action moves forward through speeches or representations rather than through narration.

	actors	The people who portray the characters in the play
	script	The written version of the play that contains both the actors' lines and stage directions to guide their movements on the stage
	act	A division of the action in the play. Most plays follow the structure of five acts.
	scene	A smaller division of the action within an act. Scene changes occur when groups of characters enter and exit the stage to deliver their lines.
	dialogue	The lines that characters say as they speak to one another. Since there is no narrator in a play, the dialogue is how the audience gets to know each character. If a character delivers lines while alone on stage, this is a monologue or soliloquy. It serves to let the audience know an individual character's thoughts and feelings.
	stage	The flat surface, often raised higher than the audience, on which the actors act out the play. There is usually a curtain in front that closes between acts.
	set	The set often includes a backdrop with painted scenery and some kind of furniture, trees, or shrubbery.
	theater	The building in which the play is performed. A completely outdoor theater is known as an amphitheater.
	costumes	Clothing worn by the actors to help them represent the characters
	props	Items, such as swords or flowers, that help the audience to visualize the action

THEMES CHART

COMMON THEMES	☐	forgiveness, redemption, teamwork, good versus evil, power of love, growing up, courage, family, perseverance, justice, kindness
What is the **THEME**?	☐	What message does the end of the story emphasize?
	☐	Did the characters in this story learn a lesson? Did you?
How does the theme affect the **CHARACTERS**?	☐	What sacrifices does the main character make? How does this change the character?
	☐	Do the characters have conversations about the theme?
	☐	What could you celebrate about what happened to or for the characters?
How does the **SETTING** support the theme?	☐	Does the setting reflect the theme? Are there contrasts between light and dark? Growth and decay?
How does the **CONFLICT** support the theme?	☐	How does the resolution of the conflict illustrate the theme?
How does the **PLOT** support the theme?	☐	How do the actions of the story contribute to the lessons learned?
FOOD FOR THOUGHT	☐	Is the author trying to reveal a truth about human nature using the theme? What? How?
	☐	What Bible stories or characters exemplify this theme? What other stories that you know show this theme?
	☐	How does this theme answer the questions *What is a good life?*, *What is a good death?*, *What is true love?*

LITERATURE

SERVING SUGGESTION: At the school table, at the dinner table, at the coffee table, or at the picnic table

PREP TIME: 10 minutes

INGREDIENTS: Document Annotation Chart (at right); highlighters or colored pencils and paper (or whiteboard and markers); history sentence or sentence from a reference book

STEPS:

1. Choose two history memory work sentences from your *Foundations Curriculum* or create two of your own. Here's an example from the guide:

   In 1773, colonists disguised as Mohawks dumped tea from the British East India Company into the Boston Harbor.

2. Decide as a family how you'd like to mark the *who, what, when,* and *where* part of the sentence. It could be with different colors or symbols. A few ideas for symbols are:

   - For *when,* a circle with a very simple clock face.

   - For *where,* a circle with compass markings.

   - For *what* happened, a circle with an exclamation mark.

   - For *who,* a circle with eyes.

3. Write the sentence in large script. As you read it, have your learners circle the fact with the assigned color or label it with a symbol. Practice again with your other sentence.

4. Now for the fun! Ask all the family members to create their own history sentence. The sentence can be about a special family memory or something silly. Be sure to include the *who, what, when,* and *where.*

5. Exchange history sentences with a partner and label them with colors or symbols. Have fun recounting just the facts!

YIELD: Conscious readers who begin to identify and mark key facts in a short passage

TIPS AND HINTS

Through history, we see God's unfolding plan for humanity. We learn about both the incredible triumphs and the dismal failures of humankind. As American historian David McCullough wrote: "History is a guide to navigation in perilous times. History is who we are and why we are the way we are." We read and remember so that we may, in turn, act wisely.

Most of us do not need to be persuaded to study history the way we might need to be convinced to study fine arts or Latin, but we need clear direction on how to study history classically. For the grammar student (ages 4–11), the answer is twofold: young students need to memorize and recite key information, and they need to be delighted by good stories. This memorization prepares grammar students to move into the dialectic years (ages 12–13), when they begin to analyze historical events. Learning the stories of history not only builds core knowledge but also activates and exercises students' imagination, which will then become fully engaged during the rhetoric (or poetic) years (ages 14–18).

DOCUMENT ANNOTATION CHART

Reading hard things like historical documents involves action—the act of marking the document. Try a few annotation methods, or variations of methods, until you find one that you like, one that helps you engage with the text and the ideas of the author. Here's a method that only requires a pen or pencil.

MARK	WHAT	WHERE	WHEN
underscore	Major point here!	text	For major points or important or forceful statements
circles	This is important to note!	text	For major points or important or forceful statements
vertical lines	//	margin	To emphasize an important passage
star or asterisk	*	margin	Use sparingly to emphasize the ten or twenty most important statements in the book. Consider folding the bottom or top corner of every page where such marks are used.
numbers	Point #1, 2a, 2b, 3 . . .	text; margin	To indicate a sequence of points the author makes in developing a single argument
numbers	See page 12 for another example.	margin	To indicate where else in the book the author made points relevant to the point marked; to tie up the ideas in a book that are separated by many pages but belong together
notes	Why does the author mention this here?	margin; top/bottom of page	For summarizing key points or recording questions a passage raises in your mind; reducing a complicated discussion to a simple statement; recording the sequence of major points through the books
more notes	The background to this story is . . .	front-end and back-end papers	To make notes on those blank pages in the front and back of the book for which no one knows the purpose

How to Read a Book by Mortimer J. Adler and Charles Van Doren. New York: Simon and Schuster, 1972. Print.

The Magna Carta 1215

(20) For a trivial offence, a free man shall be fined only in proportion to the degree of his offence, and for a serious offence correspondingly, but not so heavily as to deprive him of his livelihood. In the same way, a merchant shall be spared his merchandise, and a villein the implements of his husbandry, if they fall upon the mercy of a royal court. None of these fines shall be imposed except by the <u>assessment on oath of reputable men</u> of the neighbourhood. *See para. 4*

(21) Earls and barons shall be fined only by their equals, and in proportion to the gravity of their offence.

* (22) A fine imposed upon the lay property of a clerk in holy orders shall be assessed upon the same principles, without reference to the value of his ecclesiastical benefice.

(23) No town or person shall be forced to build bridges over rivers except those with an ancient obligation to do so. *Directed against the misuse developed for hunting falcons and hawks*

(24) No sheriff, constable, coroners, or other royal officials are to hold lawsuits that should be held by the royal justices. *Subdivision of a county*

(25) Every county, hundred, wapentake, and tithing shall remain at its ancient rent, without increase, except the royal demesne manors.

As students begin to read and study difficult documents (historical records, ancient literature, detailed scientific journals), a habit and method of marking a text becomes a great learning tool.

LITERATURE

SERVING SUGGESTION: Riding in the car, while finishing breakfast, or relaxing on the porch

PREP TIME: 5 minutes

INGREDIENTS: Rhetorical Devices Chart (at right), simple understanding of alliteration, a good imagination

STEPS:
1. Explain alliteration to your children. Give examples of words that have the same beginning sounds: *cats*, *cars*, *caps*. Your examples may be all verbal, or you may choose to write them down so that children see the repeated common first letter. Do several sets of words, asking them for suggestions.

2. Now, suggest choosing one word that can be described, like "pig." Can you and your children think of two more words that begin with "p" that could describe "pig"? What about "**pretty, pink pig**"? How delightfully descriptive! Much more fun to say—and more memorable too.

3. Have each child try to think of two adjectives to describe himself, adjectives that begin with the sound at the beginning of his name. (Strong, smiling Seth or tall, tanned Tabitha)

4. Take turns finding things you can see to describe alliteratively! Then, try something you cannot see but can name such as "sweet, soft singing" or "hot, humid holidays."

5. Try identifying alliteration in the books and stories you read; remember, the words don't have to be right next to each other to make an impact, just nearby.

YIELD: A student whose ear is attuned to lyrical expression and who recognizes how to create the memorable phrases others will find arresting. Students' ears will be tickled by alliteration as you share read-alouds and as they read independently. Understanding this literary device will grow through formal writing programs in the Challenge years, building on the introduction given during the Essentials program.

TIPS AND HINTS

When you and your student learn to recognize and appreciate rhetorical devices such as alliteration, you become better readers. When you learn to use them, you become better writers. Becoming a persuasive writer means learning to invite a reader's senses into your communication; you can appeal to the ears, eyes, mind, and heart of your reader and speak more movingly. Consider how poetry moves us by painting memorable word pictures. *Through wisdom is an house builded; and by understanding it is established: And by knowledge shall the chambers be filled with all precious and pleasant riches* (Proverbs 24:3–4).

GRAMMAR OF
ARITHMETIC

GRAMMAR OF
ARITHMETIC

"Consistent study habits are
the most important part of
learning math."
—Leigh Bortins, *The Core* (134)

Choosing This Course: **WHY** study arithmetic

- We want our children to see the order and harmony of God's created world and to understand that He has revealed that order and harmony to us in the language of mathematics; we want our children to speak God's language!
- In practical terms, we want our children to be equipped to manage their own homes and budgets, use mathematical laws and formulas to solve daily issues, and be able to think conceptually about the world.

Basic Ingredients: **WHAT** kind of arithmetic to study

- "The main goal of arithmetic, which is the grammar of mathematics, is developing computational skills and memorization of basic laws and formulas."
  —Leigh Bortins, *The Core* (133)
- We know children need to learn about numbers, operations, and laws. We also want them to know shapes, patterns, place value, and measurement.
- Children should learn the "language" of math: symbols, sentence structures, and rules.
- These beginning concepts are pre-skills for algebra and calculus; skill mastery comes before abstract application that higher level math requires.

Learning to Cook: **HOW** to become mathematicians

- We need to "play with numbers" as we have learned to play with words; in this way we will reclaim math education as we have reclaimed reading! Make time to notice the numbers, shapes, and patterns all around you; find the wonder of math in the things you see.
- Slow down, work on memorizing math facts for speed and accuracy and discuss numbers, operations, and laws for understanding.
- Consistent study habits and practice are the most important parts of learning math. Daily lessons, over-practicing concepts, neatness in presentation, checking answers, explaining equations, and ordering steps of each problem are the habits you want to begin early and continue into high school.

Raising Chefs: **BECOMING LIFELONG LEARNERS**

- With our littlest learners, we are building foundations: sort of like filling a pantry with quality ingredients so that we have on hand everything we could need to create amazing meals and festive celebrations. In arithmetic, we teach them to count, write numerals, do simple operations, recognize shapes and patterns, and measure all sorts of things using various units and tools.
- As children develop, they are ready to combine those basic ingredients in new ways, eager to see what happens. In arithmetic, they learn to translate word problems into equations, use the laws and formulas they've memorized to solve equations, and begin to think in more abstract ways about the math they see all around them.
- As children become older mathematicians, we show them how the laws and formulas they know can be applied in innovative ways to solve a problem, express beauty, or teach truth to another.

	Build a foundation of **KNOWLEDGE** (Grammar)	Make connections for **UNDERSTANDING** (Dialectic)	Act with **WISDOM** (Rhetoric)
ARITHMETIC	• Name the numerals 1–100; recognize them and write them. • Attend to where we see numbers (calendar, clock, price tags, books, recipes). • Name the symbols you see in math equations. Name the tokens we use for money. Learn to count money. • Express numbers in different forms. • Use math equations to "tell a story."	• Define the laws that govern mathematical processes; learn to use these laws to solve equations. • Compare different types of numbers, and learn to translate between forms. • Work on translating words into numbers and symbols to solve word problems. • Consider circumstances when solving equations, and learn to choose correct procedures.	• Work on using knowledge and understanding to solve increasingly complex problems. • Master complex math, such as trigonometry and calculus, by building on your math understanding. • Seek out beauty in nature, finding the math in God's creation.

The Challenge of Arithmetic: **WHEN** you are ready for more

- The charts and activities in this guide are designed to help parents begin building the math skills young children need. Learning to recognize and write numbers, identify patterns and shapes, take simple measurements, and do simple calculations are the basic ingredients in a math education.
- Recognizing different types of numbers (counting numbers, integers, fractions, decimals, percents . . .) and practicing all the operations (addition, subtraction, multiplication, division, exponents, and roots) on all types of numbers equips students to tackle more complex and abstract math as they develop. Students with a firm grasp on the basics are well-prepared for algebra, geometry, trigonometry, and calculus.

TOOLS FOR EVERY AGE

	SCRIBBLERS		FOUNDATIONS/ESSENTIALS		CHALLENGE
☐	manipulatives (beans, Cheerios)	☐	math card games	☐	protractor
☐	counting blocks/cubes	☐	decks of cards	☐	compass
☐	easy workbooks	☐	dice	☐	scientific calculator
☐	ruler	☐	workbooks	☐	graphing calculator
☐	coins for counting	☐	*Tables, Squares & Cubes*	☐	ruler
☐	clock	☐	*Quick Flip Arithmetic*	☐	notebook
☐	scale	☐	math flashcards	☐	colored pens/pencils
☐	measuring cups and spoons	☐	ruler	☐	charts (functions, formulas . . .)

ARITHMETIC

SERVING SUGGESTION: On the floor or at the table

PREP TIME: 5 minutes

INGREDIENTS: Hundred Chart (at right; consider copying this chart and placing it in a page protector); a dry erase marker

STEPS: Find the patterns in counting by becoming familiar with the Hundred Chart.

1. Find all the odd numbers. If page-protected, your child can use a marker and mark the numbers in some way.

2. Find the even numbers.

3. Find numbers ending in zero.

4. Find numerals with a "1," then "2"; then discuss whether the numerals are in the ones or tens place. You can do this for all the numerals.

5. Have your child guess a secret number using the Twenty Questions format with just yes or no as an answer. They are not allowed to guess the secret number until all twenty questions have been asked. Your child can ask questions like "Is your secret number odd?" If the answer is no, your child now knows the secret number is even. Your child can cross out all the odd numbers on the Hundred Chart.

6. For younger children, sing the Foundations Skip Counting song while your little learner points to the number sung. Older children can time themselves as they mark all the prime numbers.

7. What other patterns does your child find?

YIELD: Awareness that mathematicians seek order

TIPS AND HINTS

The classical model of education includes arithmetic rather than algebra as an art of learning; we begin building a foundation with the basics in order to establish a firm footing for later mathematical thinking. The more time your children spend "playing with numbers," the more deftly they will manipulate the numbers later as they solve equations and decipher math mysteries. Weak arithmetic skills lead to weak algebra skills because algebra is mainly the replacement of numbers with letters. If you can't quickly and accurately calculate with numbers, it is hard to see the relationships between abstract letters in algebra. Quick, accurate calculations allow the brain to focus on the algebraic relationships rather than be distracted by unfamiliar patterns.

The Hundred Chart, as well as the multiplication tables, introduces children to the patterns of calculation; once they master these patterns with counting numbers, they will be able to recognize and use these same patterns to manipulate complex fractions, percents, quadratic equations, and more.

HUNDRED CHART

1	2	3	4	5	6	7	8	9	10
11	12	13	14	15	16	17	18	19	20
21	22	23	24	25	26	27	28	29	30
31	32	33	34	35	36	37	38	39	40
41	42	43	44	45	46	47	48	49	50
51	52	53	54	55	56	57	58	59	60
61	62	63	64	65	66	67	68	69	70
71	72	73	74	75	76	77	78	79	80
81	82	83	84	85	86	87	88	89	90
91	92	93	94	95	96	97	98	99	100

TOOLS TO MEASURE TIME CHART

Clocks show hours (shorter hand), minutes (longer hand), and seconds (optional sweep hand).

Analog (Face) 12-Hour Clock	Analog 24-Hour Clock
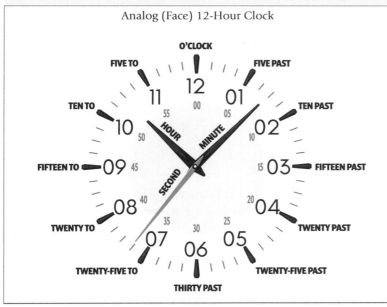	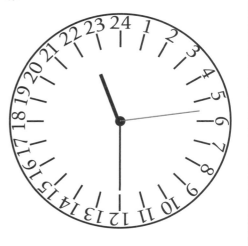
12-hour clocks make two revolutions in one day.	24-hour clocks make one revolution in one day.
AM (or a.m.): ante meridiem, before noon (morning) PM (or p.m.): post meridiem, after noon	AM and PM are not used.
Noon: 12 o'clock (day - PM) Midnight: 12 o'clock (night - AM)	Convert 24-hour time to 12-hour time by subtracting 12 hours if the hours are greater than 12. 22:15 – 12:00 = 10:15 PM.
Digital 12-Hour Clock	Digital 24-Hour Clock

Calendars show years, months, weeks and days.

A **timeline** is a display of a list of events in chronological order. It is typically a long bar labeled with dates.

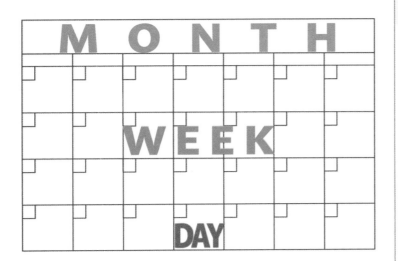

Christ separates Old Testament (BC) from New Testament (AD) times.

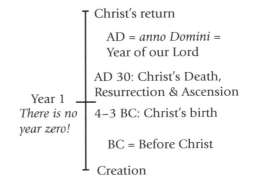

Christ's return

AD = *anno Domini* = Year of our Lord

AD 30: Christ's Death, Resurrection & Ascension

4–3 BC: Christ's birth

Year 1
There is no year zero!

BC = Before Christ

Creation

ARITHMETIC

SERVING SUGGESTION: Outside in the dirt, snow, or sand

PREP TIME: 5 minutes

INGREDIENTS: Unit Circle Chart (at right), feet, string, book, and yardstick

STEPS:

1. Have your child outline a circle in the dirt, snow, or sand by holding his heel still and pivoting around; clear the interior of the space.

2. Using the yardstick and a drawing stick, draw one line that cuts the circle in half horizontally and one that cuts it vertically. Identify these lines as the *x*-axis and *y*-axis.

3. Place the book in the angle formed by the two lines to demonstrate that the angle measures 90 degrees and is a right angle?

4. Using the foot as a measuring device, cut two pieces of string for the circle, one the length of the shoe and the other half the length of the shoe.

5. Encourage your child to use the two pieces of string and the yardstick (as the third side) to form triangles anywhere on the circle.

6. Now work together to see how many triangles you can form that follow all of these rules:
   - One angle must touch the center of the circle where the *x*-axis and *y*-axis cross.
   - One line must touch the center and the edge is the circle.
   - One angle must be a right angle.
   - One line must lie on top of the *x*-axis.

YIELD: A sense of discovery and fun with foundational mathematics

TIPS AND HINTS

Math tastes great! Sometimes as parents we let our own childhood fears and frustrations flavor how we present mathematics. But math can be a treat when you help your children to celebrate the order of our Creator and His handiwork by making observations and comparisons using numbers. All children can learn to love math, as it matches their natural inclination to find patterns. In the early years, math can be playing with numbers, drawing shapes and lines, discovering patterns, and observing relationships. Once your children develop a taste for math, they will develop a more sophisticated palate and be ready to dig into the "meat" of the why and the how.

UNIT CIRCLE CHART

The colored triangles in the unit circle are repetitions of 30°-60°-90° and 45°-45°-90° triangles.

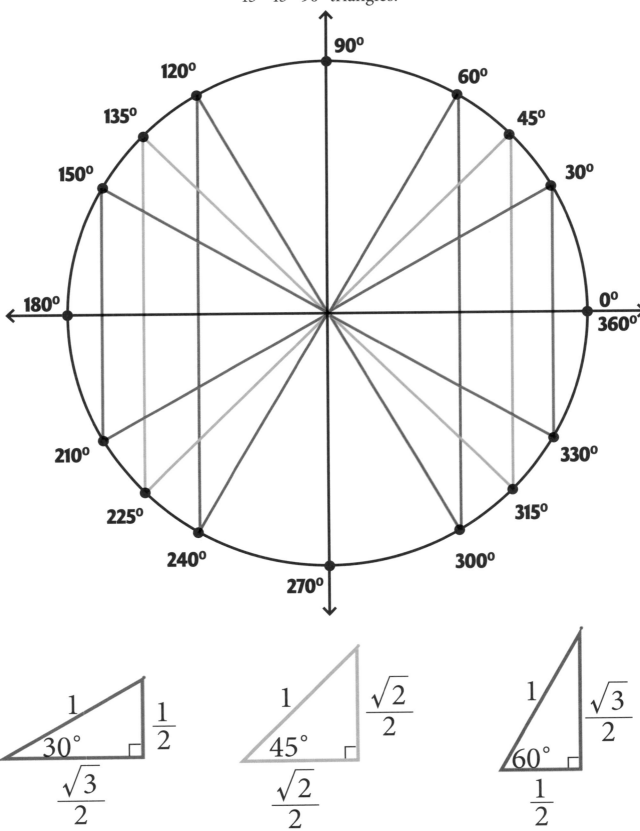

ARITHMETIC

SERVING SUGGESTION: At the playground, while waiting for siblings to finish soccer practice, or at the table in the kitchen

PREP TIME: 5 minutes

INGREDIENTS: *XY* Chart (at right); nut, small candy, or pebble

STEPS:

1. In order to become familiar with this math tool, take a look at the *XY* Chart together and ask "what do you see?" questions. (You can discuss the lines in the center of the graph and how the horizontal line is marked "X" and the vertical line is marked "Y." Point out that the intersection point in the middle is called the "origin" and for counting purposes is "0." Notice that the "X" and "Y" lines divide the figure into four equal squares known as quadrants. Notice that the quadrants are numbered with Roman numerals. Are there squares in every quadrant? Count the squares with your children; are there an equal number in each quadrant/quarter of the graph?

2. To practice how to read graphs and identify points, have your children place a rock (or a nut or candy if it is snack time) in a few of the squares. Then ask them to count over and up or down from the origin. How many **over** did they hop? (This moves you along the *x*-axis.) How many squares **up** or **down** from the origin? (This moves you along the *y*-axis.)

3. Because we record points as ordered pairs, and in the same order every time, we note the "*x*" value first in the ordered pair and the "*y*" value second. An almond or candy placed in the square 3 over from the origin and then 2 up would be at (3, 2). (For older children, you can bring in the idea of negative values as those to the left of the origin on the *x*-axis or below the origin on the *y*-axis.)

4. Give your children a point, like (3, 3), and ask them to put a pebble on that point. You can play this lots of times, inside or outside! You can even use "grids" you find around your neighborhood: hopscotch boards, brick sidewalks, concrete patio pavers, and tiles on a floor. Use checkered tablecloths in restaurants to place water glasses until the food arrives!

5. Also use these common grids to calculate area. If there is a 3×4 grid (floor tiles, squares on a tablecloth), your youngest children can count 1, 2, . . . 12 to find the total squares—the area. Older children can say there are $3 \times 4 = 12$. The area would be the number of units of length times the number of units of width; in this example, the area of this grid would be 12:3 units (tiles) times 4 units (tiles) equals 12.

6. When you are attending to the "grids" you discover around your neighborhood, remind your children that an architect, contractor, or concrete- or brick-maker had to figure out the number of squares and the area to build the buildings, streets, and sidewalks. Many jobs require math.

YIELD: A child who is gradually becoming familiar with the rectangular coordinate plane! By introducing the ideas slowly, your child will gradually understand concepts such as the number line, graphing points on a plane, calculating area, measuring angles, and the slopes of lines. Many "higher math" concepts are built around this simple chart.

TIPS AND HINTS

Ordered pairs represent "functions" in math. Functions mimic our relationship with God and people. Think of God on the *y*-axis and people on the *x*-axis: (x, y) = (people, God). Can we relate to people exclusive of God? No, because even the point (4, 0) acknowledges that the *y*-axis exists. Can we relate to God exclusive of people? No, because even the point (0, 4) acknowledges that the *x*-axis exists.

XY CHART

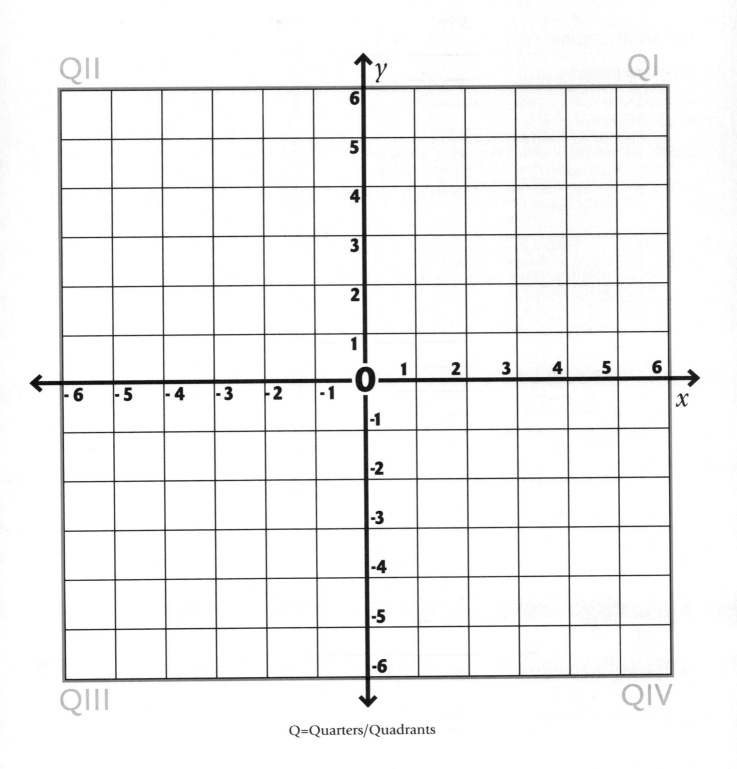

Q=Quarters/Quadrants

ARITHMETIC

SERVING SUGGESTION: Kitchen table, coffee table, school table, or paved driveway

PREP TIME: 5 minutes

INGREDIENTS: Polygons Chart (at right), polygon pattern blocks, tessellation coloring books (optional), long paper, colored pencils

STEPS:

1. To become more familiar with polygons and their characteristics, count the sides and angles of polygons like the ones on the facing chart.

2. As you go about your daily activities, look for these shapes and name them. Find the squares and rectangles in the packaging at the grocery store, and the triangles and octagons in traffic signs. Choose a shape and have your child point out all examples of the "shape of the day." Practice drawing shapes on paper, on the driveway, or in the sand.

3. Remember that play is about more than having fun for your littlest learners! When you play with blocks (Lego bricks or other types), have your children note the shape of each block and the shapes they can make by combining blocks. Can they match a creation of yours? Can you mimic one of theirs?

4. When you play blocks with your children, create repeating patterns with the blocks. You can use shapes or colors to create the patterns (blue, purple, green, blue, purple . . .). Ask your child: "What block do you think goes next?" Recognizing patterns builds spatial awareness, observation skills, and critical thinking skills.

5. Put the pattern blocks on paper and trace around the patterns. Have older children trace a few types to make tessellations. Tessellations are created when one or more shapes (or tiles) are repeated over and over again covering a given area without any gaps or overlaps. A simple tessellation is a checkerboard. Look into the art of M. C. Escher for some examples!

6. Use tessellation coloring books to entertain children in quiet places. Tessellations teach children about translations, reflections, and rotations.

YIELD: A child aware of geometric patterns who will be more comfortable with transformations in the study of geometry later on; a person with spatial awareness who will be a better packer, a more able pattern identifier, and a more appreciative art observer. Your child will study shapes and patterns going forward in mathematics, music, and art.

TIPS AND HINTS

Tessellations are a bridge to Eastern art like the art that often decorates Muslim architecture. For older students, this could open a conversation about the commandment "make no graven images" from Exodus 20, and the Eastern versus Western interpretation of that Scripture.

POLYGONS CHART

	Name	Shape	Vertices	Triangles	Diagonals	Σ Interior ∠'s	1 Interior ∠	1 Exterior ∠	Σ Exterior ∠'s
TRIANGLES	Equilateral		3	1	0	180°	60°	120°	360°
	Isosceles		3	1	0	180°	60°	120°	360°
	Scalene		3	1	0	180°	60°	120°	360°
	Right		3	1	0	180°	60°	120°	360°
QUADRILATERALS	Trapezoid		4	2	2	360°	90°	90°	360°
	Rhombus		4	2	2	360°	90°	90°	360°
	Rectangle		4	2	2	360°	90°	90°	360°
	Square		4	2	2	360°	90°	90°	360°
POLYGONS	Pentagon		5	3	5	540°	108°	72°	360°
	Hexagon		6	4	9	720	120°	60°	360°
	Heptagon		7	5	12	900	128.57...°	51.42...°	360°
	Octagon		8	6	20	1080	135°	45°	360°
	Nonagon		9	7	27	1260	140°	40°	360°
	Decagon		10	8	35	1440	144°	36°	360°

ARITHMETIC

SERVING SUGGESTION: On the floor

PREP TIME: 5 minutes

INGREDIENTS: Yardstick or meter stick

STEPS:
1. On a yardstick, mark one foot and 1.6 feet so that you can easily refer to these measurements.

2. Move around your house or yard, choosing some cabinets, windows, arbors, bookcases, trellises, and other decorative objects to study; do any seem more "beautiful" to you than others?

3. After you and your child identify your "beautiful things," use your yardstick to measure both the lengths and widths of your chosen objects; write them as ratios. For example, a bookcase might be six feet tall and nine feet wide, 6:9. Measure how many 1's in one direction (length, perhaps) and how many 1.6's in the other direction (width, perhaps.). If it's the same number, then the object is in the golden ratio!

4. Talk to your child about the **golden ratio** (see the diagram below), and look together at a photo of the Taj Mahal. What is beautiful about this structure? Evaluate the proportions of the building, and discuss how the proportions bring harmony or beauty.

5. Are there structures in your home or in your town that feel more attractive to you without your knowing why? It's probably because the proportion of length to width is close to the 1.618 of the golden ratio. Get a sense of this proportion and then look at your home from various angles. Learn to see the golden ratio as you drive around town and look at beautiful architecture, or try to figure out why some art work doesn't feel quite right.

6. With older children, try imposing the golden spiral on some famous works of art, like the *Mona Lisa* painting. Do you find the golden ratio in these works of art?

YIELD: A person aware of three-dimensional design and of what is considered "classically beautiful" based on proportion

TIPS AND HINTS

Sometimes a beautiful home looks funny from a certain position. That's because the original builder did not pay attention to the golden ratio, also called the "divine proportion" or phi. With a history dating back to the Egyptians and Greeks, phi is visible in classical architecture and other significant works of art. The Taj Mahal is one of the most famous examples of a building built according to the golden ratio as shown by this overlaid golden spiral.

POLYHEDRONS CHART

Pyramids	Prisms	Platonic Solids
Lateral area (LA) = $\frac{1}{2}$ (base perimeter)(height of side) **Surface Area** (SA) = LA + Area$_{base}$ **Volume** (V)= $\frac{1}{3}$ Area$_{base}$ × height *Right pyramids only*	**Lateral area** (LA) = (perimeter of the base)(height) **Surface Area** = LA + 2 Area$_{base}$ **Volume** = Area$_{base}$ × height	SA = $\sqrt{3}\,a^2$ V = $\frac{a^3}{6\sqrt{2}}$ Tetrahedron
Equilateral Triangular base	Cube	SA = $6\,(a)^2$ V = a^3 Hexahedron = Cube
Isosceles Triangular Pyramid	Rectangular Prism	SA = $2\sqrt{3}\,a^2$ V = $\frac{\sqrt{2}}{3}a^3$ Octahedron
Scalene Triangular Pyramid	Rhombus	
Right Triangular Pyramid	Parallelogram	SA = $3\sqrt{25+10\sqrt{5}}\,a^2$ V = $\frac{15+7\sqrt{5}}{4}a^3$ Dodecahedron
Acute Triangular Pyramid	Kite	SA = $5\sqrt{3}\,a^2$ V = $\frac{5(3+\sqrt{5})}{12}a^3$ Icosahedron
Obtuse Triangular Pyramid	Trapezoid	

NUMBER KNOCKOUT BOARD CHART

1	2	3	4	5	6
7	8	9	10	11	12
13	14	15	16	17	18
19	20	21	22	23	24
25	26	27	28	29	30
31	32	33	34	35	36

ARITHMETIC

SERVING SUGGESTION: Backyard or anywhere outside

PREP TIME: 5 minutes

INGREDIENTS: Chalk in different colors

STEPS:

1. People are continually presented with data, but data are often better understood when it is arranged it in a way that makes sense. Talk to your children about collecting data from your own backyard. Brainstorm the types of living things that can be seen in your yard (insects, spiders, butterflies, birds, lizards, frogs, cats, dogs, etc.). Discuss some expectations: Which animal do you most expect to see? Which animal do you least expect to see? Draw a different colored circle for each animal (or draw its shape) on the sidewalk, patio, driveway, or fence, and write its name inside the circle. Allow your child to roam the yard, looking and listening for the different animals. Use the chalk to keep count inside each circle.

    Look Up: What animals can be seen or heard in the sky, in the trees, on a fence or wire, on the rooftop, or anywhere above eye level?

    Look Down: What animals can be seen or heard on the ground?

    Look Around: What animals can be seen or heard climbing a fence or tree, flying around the flower garden, or buzzing about your ears?

2. With two or more children, you can assign them to different parts of the yard to conduct their count (one in the front yard and one in the backyard; one on the north side and one on the south side; one close to the house and one farther away, etc.).

3. Count the total number of animals in each category and make a bar graph to diagram your results. Which animal had the most counts? Which animal had the least? Did the results meet your expectations? Why or why not?

YIELD: Children who understand the concept of categorical data and the visual tools that help to represent and interpret that data

TIPS AND HINTS

Nature—and the data we collect about it—is not stagnant, but ever-changing. This activity can be repeated for each season of the year, allowing children to see patterns, make comparisons, and draw conclusions about the types of animals seen over time. Children are led from inquiry to discovery and back to wonder as they marvel at the glory and complexity of creation.

DATA ARRANGEMENT CHART

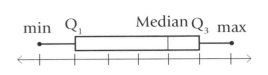

Box and Whisker Diagram

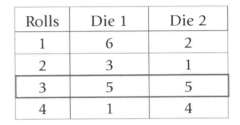

Table

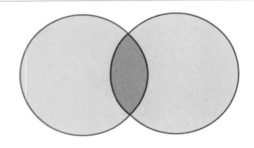

Venn Diagram

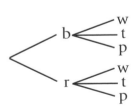

Tree Diagram

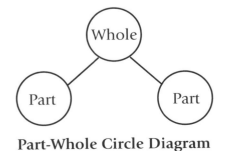

Part-Whole Circle Diagram

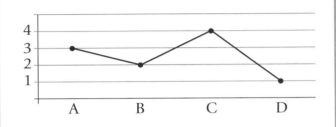

Bar Graph

Line Graph

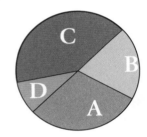

A 30%, B 20%,
C 40%, D 10%

Pie Chart

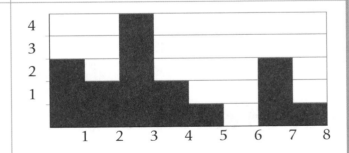

Histogram

	B₁	B₂	B₃	B₄
A₁				
A₂				

Array

GRAMMAR OF
LATIN

LATIN ADJECTIVES CHART

Latin adjectives come in two groups or families: adjectives that use first and second declension endings and adjectives that use third declension endings (with slight variations). Because adjectives must agree with the nouns they modify, adjectives must decline in gender, number, and case, just like nouns. Compare the endings in the chart below with the noun declension chart.

	1ST AND 2ND DECLENSION			3RD DECLENSION		
	masculine	feminine	neuter	masculine	feminine	neuter
	altus, alta, altum — high, deep			*fortis, forte* — brave, strong		
Cases	singular			singular		
nominative	alt**us**	alt**a**	alt**um**	fort**is**	fort**is**	fort**e**
genitive	alt**i**	alt**ae**	alt**i**	fort**is**	fort**is**	fort**is**
dative	alt**o**	alt**ae**	alt**o**	fort**i**	fort**i**	fort**i**
accusative	alt**um**	alt**am**	alt**um**	fort**em**	fort**em**	fort**e**
ablative	alt**o**	alt**a**	alt**o**	fort**i**	fort**i**	fort**i**
	plural			plural		
nominative	alt**i**	alt**ae**	alt**a**	fort**es**	fort**es**	fort**ia**
genitive	alt**orum**	alt**arum**	alt**orum**	fort**ium**	fort**ium**	fort**ium**
dative	alt**is**	alt**is**	alt**is**	fort**ibus**	fort**ibus**	fort**ibus**
accusative	alt**os**	alt**as**	alt**a**	fort**es**	fort**es**	fort**ia**
ablative	alt**is**	alt**is**	alt**is**	fort**ibus**	fort**ibus**	fort**ibus**

Latin adjectives must match the noun they modify in gender, number, and case. This rule is reflected in the endings.

Here are a few examples:

murus altus	the high wall
Porta est alta.	The gate is high.
Rex militem fortem laudat.	The king praises the brave soldier.

In Latin, the adjectives usually come after the noun they modify, but there are also many instances where the adjective comes before the noun or in another part of the sentence.

SERVING SUGGESTION: The couch

PREP TIME: 5 minutes

INGREDIENTS: Latin Personal Pronouns Chart (at right); 8 Parts of Speech Chart pronoun section (page 63)

STEPS:
1. Chant the definition of a pronoun three times with your child.

2. Tell the children a story with *no* pronouns in it: Mommy got out of bed this morning. Mommy made Mommy's bed. Mommy poured Mommy some coffee. Mommy dressed Mommy. Mommy made breakfast for Mommy's children, etc.

3. Ask your children what was silly about the story?

4. Go back and replace some of the nouns with pronouns: Mommy got out of bed. She made her bed. She poured herself some coffee. Mommy dressed herself. She made breakfast for her children, etc.

5. Allow the children to try steps 2–4 by telling a story about their day.

6. Later in the week, read through a short picture book and replace all of the pronouns with proper nouns. Discuss how it sounds.

YIELD: Children prepared for future study of personal pronouns, which will help them become better readers and writers

TIPS AND HINTS

Repeat the pronoun definition three times a day this week.

Our word "pronoun" comes from the Latin words *pro nomen*, which means "for a name." The preposition *pro* in Latin can also mean "on behalf of." Consider how many of Jesus' works are on behalf of us. He died, rose, and is at the right hand of the Father interceding on our behalf.

Once again, our grammar activity centers on something that your children already know how to use. Since they have begun speaking, they know that "she" can be used in place of "Lily," or "he" can be used in place of "Trey." Now you are calling their attention to another level of understanding: they are naming the definition of a pronoun, and they are attending to how those pronouns can be used to replace nouns in our conversation, in our writing, and in our reading.

Attending to pronouns well will help children become careful writers, better readers, and capable foreign language students. Understanding antecedents—the noun that comes before a personal pronoun and the one to which it refers—is key for clear communication when we write and read. When studying inflected languages such as Latin, pronouns are embedded in word endings. For example, the pronouns "*I, you, he/she/it, we, you* (plural), *they*" correspond to the present tense verb endings, "*-o, -s, -t, -mus, -tis, -nt.*" As you attend to pronouns together, you will learn how to be good readers, writers, speakers, and thinkers.

LATIN PERSONAL PRONOUNS CHART

Case	Case Meaning	1st person	2nd person	3rd person
Singular				
				m / f / n
Nominative	*noun*	**ego** (I)	**tu** (you)	**is / ea / id** (he/she/it)
Genitive	*of the noun*	**mei** (of me)	**tui** (of you)	**eius** (of him/her/it)
Dative	*to or for the noun*	**mihi** (to or for me)	**tibi** (to or for you)	**ei** (to or for him/her/it)
Accusative	*noun*	**me** (me)	**te** (you)	**eum / eam / id** (him/her/it)
Ablative	*by or with the noun*	**me** (by or with me)	**te** (by you)	**eo / ea / eo** (by or with him/her/it)
Plural				
				m / f / n
Nominative	*noun*	**nos** (we)	**vos** (you [plural])	**ei / eae / ea** (they)
Genitive	*of the noun*	**nostri** (of us)	**vestri** (of you [plural])	**eorum / earum / eorum** (of them)
Dative	*to or for the noun*	**nobis** (to or for us)	**vobis** (to or for you [plural])	**eis** (to or for them)
Accusative	*noun*	**nos** (us)	**vos** (you [plural])	**eos / eas / ea** (them)
Ablative	*by or with the noun*	**nobis** (by or with us)	**vobis** (by or with you [plural])	**eis** (by or with them)

Note: The personal pronouns listed above are not the only Latin pronouns. Young students can begin to learn Latin pronouns with this simple list for basic Latin pronoun use.

Students will study Latin grammar in the Challenge program from Challenges A–IV.

LATIN

SERVING SUGGESTION: In the car or around the table

PREP TIME: 5 minutes (if you are making verb cards)

INGREDIENTS: A stuffed toy per player and the **Regular Verb List** (below), listed individually on index cards. Game Leader (parent, grandparent, older sibling) will call out the "tense markers" of **Present, Past, Future** as each participant takes a turn. For the on-the-go version: the verb list and imaginary friends!

STEPS:
1. Either make a set of verb cards or just use the list verbally. Here's a **Regular Verb List** (feel free to add to this one): *play, dance, walk, zip, grin, grab, bake, bump, burp, chew, clap, dream, escape, hug, itch, jump, kick, nod, open, pull, push, spill, tap, whisper, or yell.*

    (**Regular verbs** follow a regular pattern for forming a past tense verb by adding "ed" or "d." Examples are: "Yesterday, I play**ed.**" or "Yesterday, I guzzle**d.**")

2. Each player chooses a stuffed toy and names it something silly.

3. Draw a verb card or say a verb aloud.

4. Using the present tense of the verb, conjugate it aloud in the singular using the tense marker *today.* To conjugate means to give the different forms of a verb in an inflected language as they vary according to *number, person, tense, voice, mood.* Here, you will conjugate the regular verbs only in the *singular* (number) as they change in *person* (I, you, she/he/it) and *tense* (today, yesterday, tomorrow).

5. For example, *Today, I play. Today, you play. Today, [silly animal] plays.* Each person takes a turn with the verb and his own silly animal.

6. Next, using the tense marker at the beginning of the sentence, conjugate the past tense. For example, *Yesterday, I played. Yesterday, you played. Yesterday, [silly animal] played.* Ask what "tense markers" we could we have used in our first sentences (*today, yesterday, tomorrow*). See if children have noticed the regular past tense formation of English verbs (verb + "ed").

7. Then, conjugate the future tense. *Tomorrow, I will play. Tomorrow, you will play. Tomorrow, [silly animal] will play.* See if children have noticed the addition of the word "will."

8. To make it super silly, have players act out the verbs they are conjugating.

YIELD: A child who has been introduced to the idea of conjugating verbs

TIPS AND HINTS

Children often know how to conjugate verbs from simply listening to good speech patterns as they learn to talk. Paying attention to the idea of time and how verb tenses sound will become more important as children learn formal grammar rules. These rules will guide them to become better writers in English and will pave the way for them as they learn other languages, like Latin, later.

FUN FACTS ABOUT LATIN VERBS CHART

Latin verbs have conjugation, voice, mood, tense, person, and number.

CONJUGATION

There are **four** conjugations or verb families. Each conjugation uses a set of endings to show the person, number, and tense of the verb. Although the endings are the same for the most part, the base or stem may change a bit for each conjugation. Applying different endings to a verb stem is called *conjugating*.

VOICE AND MOOD

The **three moods** are indicative, subjunctive, and imperative.

Indicative – statements of fact, questions

Imperative – commands, requests

Subjunctive – wishes, statements of possibility

The **two voices** are active and passive.

Active voice shows the subject doing the action of the verb.

Passive voice shows the subject receiving the action of the verb.

TENSE

There are **six tenses** that tell when the action of the verb is occurring (present, past, future) and the duration:

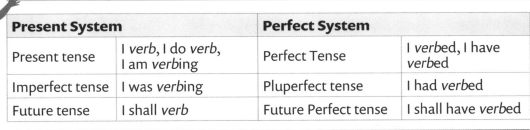

Present System		Perfect System	
Present tense	I *verb*, I do *verb*, I am *verb*ing	Perfect Tense	I *verb*ed, I have *verb*ed
Imperfect tense	I was *verb*ing	Pluperfect tense	I had *verb*ed
Future tense	I shall *verb*	Future Perfect tense	I shall have *verb*ed

PERSON AND NUMBER

There are **three persons**: 1st person, 2nd person, 3rd person and **two** classifications of **number**:

singular – one	plural – more than one
1st person – I	1st person – we
2nd person – you	2nd person – you all
3rd person – he, she, or it	3rd person – they

ROMAN RULERS AND SYMBOLS CHART

KINGS OF ROME (753 BC–509 BC)

Romulus	r. 753–715 BC	Founder of city of Rome; killed his brother, Remus, to be sole ruler
Numa Pompilius	r. 715–673 BC	Time of peace and building of temples to honor gods and goddesses
Tullus Hostilius	r. 673–642 BC	Warrior king; Rome population doubled during his reign
Ancus Marcius	r. 642–617 BC	Peaceful king; protected Rome from invaders; built great port city Ostia
Tarquinius Priscus a.k.a. Lucomo	r. 616– 578 BC	Time of great improvement and building of Rome infrastructure
Servius Tullius	r. 578–535 BC	Slave made king; continued beneficial reforms; killed by Superabus
Tarquinius Superabus a.k.a. Tarquin the Proud	r. 534–509 BC	Cruel tyrant; hated by all his people; last king of Rome

EMPERORS OF ROME

Julius Caesar	100–44 BC	Great soldier and powerful leader; ended Roman Republic as Dictator of Rome; his death precipitated a time of civil war
Augustus a.k.a. Octavian	63 BC–AD 14	Emperor of Rome at the time of the birth of Christ; began the time of the Pax Romana; good and benevolent leader
Nero	AD 37–68	Was a harsh and wicked tyrant; began persecution of Christians
Titus	AD 39–81	Sacked and destroyed Jerusalem and the Temple in AD 70; good emperor to Rome; Vesuvius erupted during his reign
Trajan	AD 53–117	A brave soldier and a good emperor; grew the Roman Empire and built many improvements to the empire
Marcus Aurelius	AD 121–180	An educated and virtuous emperor; a philosopher king; authored *Meditations*, end of Pax Romana
Diocletian	AD 245–316	Divided Roman Empire into East and West; instituted reforms of economy and government structure; final time of great persecution of Christians
Constantine I (the Great)	AD 280–337	Fought the battle of the Milvian Bridge under a Christian standard; adopted Edict of Milan, which legalized Christianity and ended persecution of Christians; reunified the empire

SYMBOLS OF ROME

fasces	A bundle of wood sticks around an axe bound together with leather thongs; a representation of supreme authority
eagle (Latin *aquila*)	The top of a Roman standard carried into battle; it was considered a disgrace to lose the standard to the enemy. Each Roman legion carried one standard
wolf (Latin *lupus*)	Representing the founding of Rome by Romulus and Remus
SPQR (Senatus Populusque Romanus)	The Senate and the People of Rome; part of standard; represents the government of ancient Roman Republic

LATIN

SERVING SUGGESTION: Any space that allows big movements

PREP TIME: 10–15 minutes

INGREDIENTS: Large box, sturdy chair, white poster board, a dowel or stick, tape, index cards, marker

STEPS:

1. Make a white cloud out of poster board and tape it to the dowel.

2. Open the lid of the box and set it on the floor next to the chair.

3. Using the Latin Prepositions and Adverbs Chart (at right), write out prepositions in both English and Latin on several cards. Some ideas to choose from are: *apud*/near, *circā*/around, *inter*/between, *in*/in, *sub*/under, *super*/over, *ante*/before. This will become your preposition deck.

4. Also make cards with the words *chair, box,* and *cloud*; make several of each. These make up your object deck.

5. Make another deck of verbs: *stand, hop, crawl, run, crawl* and others as you choose.

6. You now have a deck of prepositions, one of objects, and one of verbs.

7. Invite your family to play "In and Out, Up and Down." Each player takes a turn at being "it." Allow the other players to draw a card from each deck and direct "it" to follow directions. For example:

    crawl *sub* (under) the box;

    hop *super* (over) the cloud;

    stand *apud* (near) the chair.

8. Make sure you keep the pace quick and fun! For a challenge, draw two cards from each deck at a time and follow the directions.

Game Ideas: Older children can play Bingo or Concentration to help memorize words from the Latin Prepositions and Adverbs Chart. They will encounter these words later in their Latin studies. Challenge students can also benefit from this type of review game.

YIELD: A child who listens and follows directions; an introduction to Latin prepositions

TIPS AND HINTS

Children come in all sorts of packages. Imagine thinking of your children as gifts from God that you get to unwrap at every stage—there is always something to discover! One of the discoveries is in the area of learning styles. Some children learn best through seeing, some through hearing, and some through touching. Kinesthetic learners learn through moving! They are your wigglers, bouncers, tappers, chewers, or hoppers. Creating learning opportunities that allow for lots of wiggles keeps your learner attentive and engaged. While you are playing this game, you are helping your children to understand prepositions and how they connect nouns to other words in a sentence. This foundational understanding makes memorizing Latin prepositions and how they affect sentences easier later.

LATIN PREPOSITIONS AND ADVERBS CHART

PREPOSITIONS

IN LATIN, THE OBJECT OF THE PREPOSITION CHANGES CASE
DEPENDING ON WHICH PREPOSITION IT FOLLOWS.

TAKES THE ABLATIVE CASE

a, ab, abs - by, from

absque - without

clam - without the knowledge of

coram - before, in the presence of

cum - with

de - from, concerning

e, ex - out of, from

pro - for, instead of

sine - without

TAKES BOTH CASES

in - in

sub - up to, under

subter - under

super - over, upon

TAKES THE ACCUSATIVE CASE

ad - to

adversus, um - toward, against

ante - before

apud - at, near

circa - around

contra - against

erga - toward

extra - without, beyond

inter - between

intra - within

ADVERBS

TIME		MANNER		AFFIRMATION	
nunc	now	*bene*	well	*certe*	yes, truly
tunc	then	*male*	badly	*ita*	yes, truly
quando	when	*fortiter*	bravely	**NEGATION**	
hodie	today	*sapienter*	wisely		
heri	yesterday	*sicut*	as, like	*non*	not
cras	tomorrow				
jam	now, presently	**PLACE**		**DEGREE**	
semper	always	*ubi*	where	*satis*	enough
interdum	sometimes	*ibi*	there	*valde*	very
saepe	often	*prope*	near	*maxime*	very greatly

Memorizing vocabulary is easy for little learners with agile brains who love repetition! When your students are older and focused on learning the grammar of Latin, having so much vocabulary committed to memory will be a blessing!

LATIN

SERVING SUGGESTION: Living room floor

PREP TIME: 15 minutes

INGREDIENTS: Sticky notes, song sheet, and Conversational Latin Chart (at right)

STEPS:
1. Choose one of the listed finger plays or rhymes.
2. Substitute Latin words in the poem or song.
3. Practice singing it with the new Latin words.
4. Extend this activity by labeling familiar objects in your home with Latin words. For fun, label each other or even the family cat!

Hokey Pokey
You put your right hand (***manus***) in.
You take your right hand (***manus***) out.
You put your right hand (***manus***) in,
And you shake it all about.
You do the Hokey Pokey
And you turn yourself about.
That's what it's all about.

(Continue by putting in all the other parts of the body and finish up with your whole self!)

This Is My Family
This is my mother (***mater***), kind and dear.
(Make a fist and point to your thumb)
This is the father (***pater***), sitting near.
(Show each finger in turn)
This is the brother (***frater***), strong and tall.
This is the sister (***soror***), who plays with her ball.
This is the baby (***infans***), littlest of all.
See my whole family large and small.
(Wiggle all the fingers)

A Family Finger Play
This is a family, *(Hold up one hand, fingers spread)*
Let's count them and see,
How many there are,
And who they can be.
(Count) 1, 2, 3, 4, 5 (***unus***, ***duo***, ***tres***, ***quattuor***, ***quinque***)

This is the mother (***mater***), *(Touch pointer finger)*
Who loves everyone.
And this is the father (***pater***), *(Touch big finger)*
Who is lots of fun.

This is my sister (***soror***), *(Touch ring finger)*
She sings, and she plays.
And this is the baby (***infans***), *(Touch little finger)*
He's growing each day.

But who is this one? *(Touch thumb)*
Why it's my brother (***frater***), my friend!
And he's waiting outside,
And wants to come in! *(Knock with your hand)*

YIELD: A child who is becoming familiar with Latin words in a light-hearted way

TIPS AND HINTS
Using familiar finger plays and rhymes are great ways to introduce and practice new vocabulary. Singing is fun and keeps the task of memorizing lighthearted. A "chore, chore, chore" can become "more, more, more" with just a silly song.

CONVERSATIONAL LATIN CHART

Salve. (to one person) Salvete. (to more than one person)	Hello.
Quid agis tu?	How are you doing?
Valeo.	I am well.
Bene mihi est.	I am fine.
Gratias.	Thank you.
Deo gratias.	Thanks be to God.
Si tibi placet. (Or: Amabo te.)	Please.
Quid est nomen tibi?	What is your name?
Nomen mihi est_____.	My name is_____.
Vale. (to one person) Valete. (to more than one person)	Good-bye.

EVERYDAY WORDS

FAMILY

pater, patris	father
mater, matris	mother
frater, fratris	brother
soror, sororis	sister
filia, filiae	daughter
filius, filii	son
liberi, liberorum	children
infans, infantis	baby

BODY PARTS

caput, itis	head
collum, i	neck
auris, is	ear
nasus, i	nose
os, oris	mouth

bracchium, i	arm
manus, us	hand
crus, cruris	leg
pes, pedis	foot
oculus, i	eye

ANIMALS

feles or cattus	cat
canis	dog
avis	bird
sciurus	squirrel
piscis	fish
equus	horse

leo	lion
simia	monkey
vulpes	fox
rana	frog
lupus	wolf

Foundations students memorize Latin endings and some vocabulary; many times, that is enough to pique an interest in a new language. Challenge students will study Latin grammar and vocabulary from Challenges A –IV.

Build a foundation of **KNOWLEDGE** (Grammar)	Make connections for **UNDERSTANDING** (Dialectic)	Act with **WISDOM** (Rhetoric)
 • Name the animals, trees, and flowers in your neighborhood. • Name the great scientists and their discoveries. • Name the body systems. • Learn the classification system for living things. • Attend to the procedure for experiments. • Practice attending to details.	• Find and define the parts of whatever you are studying. • Classify any organism, using comparison to the system you have learned. • Define the parts of the scientific method. • Design an experiment to answer a question. • Consider the relationship between inventors/ scientists and the times and places in which they lived. • Use memorized formulas to solve a problem.	• Pursue beauty by studying biology, chemistry, physics, astronomy, earth science, and anatomy. • Use your growing understanding to create, discover, innovate, and invent in order to solve problems.

SCIENCE

The Challenge of Science: **WHEN** you are ready for more

As your students develop specific interests in the scientific realm, encourage them to design experiments of their own. Skills such as sketching, journaling, measuring, and writing may not seem like "science skills," but these skills will shine as students become more sophisticated science explorers.

TOOLS FOR EVERY AGE

	SCRIBBLERS		FOUNDATIONS/ESSENTIALS		CHALLENGE
☐	magnifying glass (large enough for small hands and big eyes with a stand) or hand lens	☐	thermometer	☐	dissection tools
		☐	measuring cups	☐	microscope
		☐	ruler, tape measure	☐	safety goggles
☐	tweezers	☐	water boots	☐	lab coat
☐	safety scissors	☐	small, dull knife	☐	latex gloves
☐	flashlight	☐	rock hammer	☐	lab journal
☐	funnel	☐	eye droppers	☐	nature journal
☐	bug net	☐	aquarium or fish bowl	☐	beakers and flasks
☐	bug container	☐	compass	☐	test tubes
☐	large writing notebook	☐	binoculars	☐	slides
☐	plastic bags for collections	☐	plastic collection containers	☐	measurement instruments
☐	dip net and bucket	☐	notebook or nature journal	☐	pipettes and stirring rods
☐	picture encyclopedias of the natural world	☐	colored pencils	☐	field guides
		☐	encyclopedias and science reference books	☐	trifold boards
☐		☐	field guides	☐	

SERVING SUGGESTION: Outside at a nearby park

PREP TIME: 30–45 minutes

INGREDIENTS: Nature Walk Chart (at right), keen eyes, curious mind, a bag for collectibles, water bottles, and Play-Doh or a batch of homemade salt dough (2 cups flour, 1 cup salt, 1 cup water)

STEPS:
1. Talk to your explorers about "bush eyes"; this is an encouragement to explorers everywhere to attend fully with eyes. Look up, down, under, over, and through to find what might be hidden along the path of exploration.
2. Before you head out, ask your children to think of the kinds of leaves they might see on their walk. What colors might they see? What shapes?
3. Choose a space to walk that has a few trees, grasses, or bushes.
4. Gather both green and fallen leaves.
5. At home, roll out the dough.
6. Press each leaf into the dough to make an impression.
7. Display your impressions next to each leaf.

   To extend this activity, label the type of plants from which you gathered your leaves. You can easily identify your area's leaves using the Leaf Chart (Science section, page 215).

YIELD: A family taking the opportunity to celebrate wonder in nature. Wonder is a skill to start early in your child's life. Providing your child (and yourself) with time in the natural world encourages awareness of God's "eternal power and divine nature" (Romans 1:20b NIV).

TIPS AND HINTS

"The world will never starve for want of wonders; but only for want of wonder."
—G. K. Chesterton, *Tremendous Trifles*

There is a world to introduce to your littlest learner! What a privilege to be THE ONE to point out the beauty, exquisiteness, and winsomeness in God's world. As you explore, be sure to be a wonderer yourself. You will soon find yourself as enthralled with the beauty of this world as your child.

When you plan a walk, prepare your children by anticipating what they might see and collect. This anticipation helps your little ones to intentionally attend to those details so easily overlooked. Enjoy!

NATURE WALK CHART

WHAT TO BRING

☐ Nature journal/sketchbook   ☐ Binoculars   ☐ Water
☐ Bag or container for   ☐ Magnifying glass   ☐ Snack or meal
    (non-living) specimens   ☐ Field guide

WHAT TO DO

☐ Get outside!   ☐ Explore!

HOW TO DO IT: THE FIVE CORE HABITS™ WITH NATURE-WALKING

NAMING	Identify the weather, season, environment, this plant, that animal.
ATTENDING	Use all five senses and a bit of wonder to observe details of the surroundings.
MEMORIZING	Learn the differences in plants (flowers, trees, shrubs) and animals (fish, amphibians, reptiles, birds, mammals).
EXPRESSING	Narrate, draw, or sketch the day's event, a marvelous animal, or a single leaf.
STORYTELLING	Describe the sounds (deep thunder overhead), the sights (trees bending to the wind), the action (squirrels scurrying to their homes), and the sensations (how the raindrop felt on bare heads and hands).

HOW TO LEAVE IT

☐ Put litter in its place.   ☐ Take nothing from its home.   ☐ Leave nothing but your footprints.   ☐ Keep every memory.

Use this chart to guide your family nature explorations. Practicing the Five Core Habits™ of Grammar as you go builds skills your developing students will use to explore the world through high school and beyond!

SCIENCE

SERVING SUGGESTION: Kitchen table or living room floor

PREP TIME: 20 minutes

INGREDIENTS: Wire clothes hanger, string/yarn, a variety of textured and multi-colored objects, multi-colored papers, paper towels, flavorings such as vanilla or cinnamon, or things that have a fragrance like lotion or perfume. Try to collect things that are rough, smooth, prickly, soft. Also, a couple of metal spoons. (Ideas are limitless—cotton balls, fabric, wire scrubbers, brushes, sandpaper, pine cones, empty cans . . .)

STEPS:
1. Have your child gather a pile of objects that have a variety of textures and colors.
2. Put a bit of vanilla flavoring or perfume on different paper towels or cotton balls.
3. Tie yarn onto the clothes hanger.
4. Tie the two spoons close together on the clothes hanger, so they clink together.
5. Start tying on each remaining object with the yarn.
6. Together explore each object before you tie it onto the hanger. How does it feel? Smell? Look? Can it make a sound?
7. Hang up your mobile and ask other family members or special neighbors to tickle their senses!

To extend this activity, throw a five-senses dinner and offer a variety of sour, sweet, savory, and salty foods!

YIELD: A child who recognizes the special job of each of our senses in exploring God's creation

TIPS AND HINTS

God has designed us to explore His world! He has created our bodies to be sensitive to color, movement, smell, touch, sound, taste, light. Our mouths water when we smell cookies baking. Our hearts race when we hear a loud noise. Our eyes moisten when we see a beautiful landscape. His creation is here to help us grow in our worship of Him. "The heavens declare His glory." Use this season with your family to take time to explore His world. Help your littlest learners recognize the wonders He has placed in their path and gently draw their attention to their heavenly Father who created them.

SENSES IN NATURE CHART

Stop, look, and listen . . . *and* touch, taste, and smell! A good way to be "sense-ible" with the natural world is to attend to it with the five senses: *sight, hearing, taste, smell, touch*. Looking and listening closely is part of attending, but you may need to slow down or even stop to *notice* and *compare* the finer details of the size, color, shape, texture, smell, and sound of things. Your senses can detect so many things in every realm of science. Here's a list to get even the youngest discoverer started with attending, just by stepping outside.

ASTRONOMY	**NAMES OF THE PLANETS:** Mercury, Venus, Earth, Mars, Jupiter, Saturn, Uranus, Neptune
	PHASES OF THE MOON: new, crescent, quarter, gibbous, full

PHYSICS	**MOTION:** movements of animals, movements in nature, and movements in the atmosphere
	SOUND: nature, animal, and environmental sounds
	TYPES OF ODORS: floral, woody, fruity, minty, sweet, pungent, chemical, decayed
	LIGHT: morning, daytime, evening, sunrise, sunset, dawn, dusk, sunny, cloudy

CHEMISTRY	**TASTE BUDS:** sweet, salty, sour, bitter
	TEMPERATURES: warm, hot, boiling, cool, cold, freezing
	STATES OF MATTER: solid, liquid, gas, plasma

BIOLOGY	**PARTS OF A PLANT:** leaf, stem, root, flower
	PARTS OF A FLOWER: petal, stamen, anther, pistil, sepal
	TYPES OF ANIMALS: vertebrate, invertebrate
	PARTS OF THE FOOD CHAIN: producer, consumer, decomposer
	TYPES OF CONSUMERS: herbivore, carnivore, omnivore
	KINGDOMS: animal, plant, fungi, protista, archaea, bacteria

EARTH SCIENCE	**KINDS OF ROCKS:** sedimentary, metamorphic, igneous
	LAND BIOMES: grassland, desert, scrubland, tundra, deciduous forest, coniferous forest, tropical rain forest
	AQUATIC BIOMES: ponds and lakes, streams and rivers, wetlands and estuaries, oceans and seas
	TYPES OF CLOUDS: cumulonimbus, cirrus, stratus, cumulus, stratocumulus
	FORMS OF POLLUTION: noise, air, water, land, thermal, radioactive
	TYPES OF SEASONS: fall, winter, spring, summer

MOON AND STARS CHART

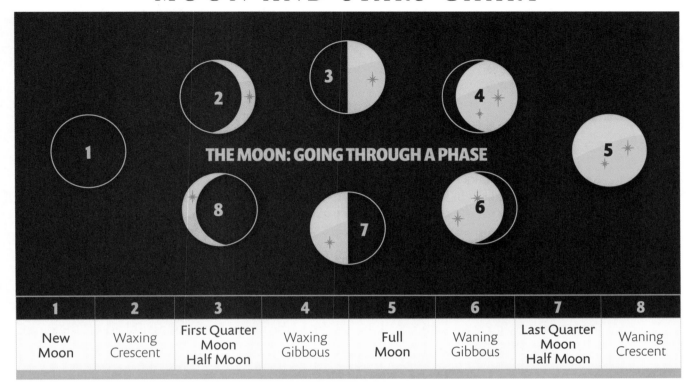

THE MOON: GOING THROUGH A PHASE

1	2	3	4	5	6	7	8
New Moon	Waxing Crescent	First Quarter Moon Half Moon	Waxing Gibbous	Full Moon	Waning Gibbous	Last Quarter Moon Half Moon	Waning Crescent

THE STARS: CONNECTING THE DOTS

	BIG DIPPER	DRACO	LITTLE DIPPER	SOUTHERN CROSS
HEMISPHERE	Northern			Southern
CONSTELLATION	Ursa Major "Great Bear"	Draco "Dragon"	Ursa Minor "Small Bear"	Crux "Southern Cross"
STARS	~7	~14	~7	~5
FEATURES	Pointer Stars	Cat's Eye Nebula	Polaris "North Star"	Coalsack molecular cloud

The two stars in the cup of the Big Dipper, farthest from the handle, are the Pointer Stars. An imaginary line drawn through them will point to the North Star.

The North Star's fixed location in the sky has made it a useful navigational tool for centuries. One is facing north when facing the North Star.

Although not fixed like the North Star, the Southern Cross helped point navigators to the south.

"And God said, Let there be lights in the firmament of the heaven to divide the day from the night; and let them be for signs, and for seasons, and for days, and years."
Genesis 1:14

Students will learn about the night sky during their Challenge B History of Astronomy semester and again in Challenge I's weather module.

SERVING SUGGESTION: Any open space

PREP TIME: 15 minutes

INGREDIENTS: Two pieces of paper, toy cars, masking tape, book or plank for a ramp, and balloon

STEPS:

1. Ask your child to take two sheets of paper and drop both at the same time. Record what happens. Now take two sheets, wad one up into a ball and keep the other as a sheet. Before dropping them, ask your child to make a prediction about which will land first. Drop both of them at the same time. What did you see? Why did this happen? Were you surprised?

2. Using toy cars, have your child roll them on different surfaces—perhaps a smooth wooden floor and a carpeted floor. Which surface allows the car to go farther? Why? How can you change things to make the car go slower? Faster?

3. Ask your little learner to design a ramp for their car. Put a piece of tape on the floor where they predict their car will stop. Roll the car down the ramp. Have your child adjust the ramp to hit the target.

4. Blow up a balloon and, before releasing it, ask your child how far it will fly. Try to make it go farther. What did you change?

YIELD: A basic understanding of scientific hypotheses and Newton's Laws

TIPS AND HINTS

Predicting outcomes is an important skill to develop especially in the areas of reading and science. It encourages learners to anticipate results by using their prior knowledge and experiences. Predictions also help our learners to focus their attention as they eagerly await results of an experiment or the end of a story. And it prepares us for the wonderful surprises that are hidden in our universe! Use part of your day to ask "What will happen next?" questions, and be open to lots of unexpected outcomes.

PHYSICS EQUATIONS AND LAWS CHART

An equation is a mathematical representation of two things that are equal. Equations are useful for solving mathematical problems, but the real "power" of an equation is its ability to give us a true and accurate description of our world.

FAMOUS PHYSICS EQUATIONS

FORMULA DEFINITION	EQUATION	UNITS OF MEASUREMENT
DENSITY = Mass ÷ Volume	$\rho = \dfrac{m}{V}$	kg/L (kilograms per liter)
PRESSURE = Force ÷ Area	$P = \dfrac{F}{A}$	Pa (pascals)
WORK = Force × Displacement	$W = Fs$	J (joules)
SPEED = Distance ÷ Time	$s = \dfrac{d}{t}$	m/s or mph (meters per second or miles per hour)
AVERAGE SPEED = Total Distance ÷ Total Time	$s_{av} = \dfrac{\Delta d}{\Delta t}$	m/s (meters per second) mph (miles per hour)
VELOCITY = Displacement ÷ Time	$v = \dfrac{\Delta x}{t}$	m/s, mph, ft/s (meters per second, miles per hour, feet per second)
ACCELERATION = Velocity ÷ Time	$a = \dfrac{\Delta v}{\Delta t}$	m/s² (meters per second squared)
POWER = Work ÷ Time	$P = \dfrac{W}{\Delta t}$	W (watts)
CENTRIPETAL FORCE = Mass × Velocity² ÷ Radius	$F_c = \dfrac{mv^2}{r}$	N (newtons)
CENTRIPETAL ACCELERATION = Velocity² ÷ Radius	$a_c = \dfrac{v^2}{r}$	m/s² (meters per second squared)
FORCE = Mass × Acceleration	$F = m \cdot a$	kgf (kilogram-force)

NEWTON'S LAWS OF MOTION

Three laws of physics that laid the foundation for the study of the motion of objects.

First Law of Motion	The Law of Inertia	An object at rest tends to stay at rest, and an object in motion tends to continue moving in a straight line at constant speed unless an outside force acts upon it.
Second Law of Motion	The Law of Acceleration	Newton's second law of motion states that force equals mass times acceleration.
Third Law of Motion	The Law of Force	For every action, there is an equal and opposite reaction.

Students begin science memory work in Foundations and become dialectic and rhetorical with their knowledge as they study physical science in Challenge I and physics in Challenge IV.

SCIENCE

SERVING SUGGESTION: Your house for a scavenger hunt!

PREP TIME: 15 minutes

INGREDIENTS: Periodic Table of the Elements Chart (at right), Element Scavenger Hunt List (below), bags for collecting, index cards for labeling, markers

STEPS:
1. God has designed our universe in a beautifully ordered way. The periodic table is a list of 118 elements that are used to create the matter of our world. In fact, most of the matter of the universe is created from the first 18 elements. Let's look for a few that are in plain sight.

2. Download and print the list for your element hunt. (Parent, you might check the list and make sure these items are around.)

3. Give each person a bag for collecting and Scavenger Hunt List (below)—the right hand column is only for older children. Ready, set, go!

4. After each person finishes the hunt, arrange the finds on the table. Use index cards to label the item and what element was used to make the object. Use the chart (at right) to find the element and write out the symbol. Did anything surprise you?

Element Scavenger Hunt List and Answer Key

Toothpaste	(Fluoride)
Sand	**(Silicon)**
Aluminum Foil	(Aluminum)
Salt	**(Sodium and Chloride)**
Water	(Hydrogen and Oxygen)
Nickels/ Utensils	**(Nickel)**
Nails	(Iron)
Seashells	**(Calcium)**
Banana	(Potassium)
Green Leaf	**(Magnesium)**
Jewelry	(Gold or Silver)
Canned Foods	**(Steel)**
Pencils	(Carbon)
Battery	**(Lithium)**
Paper	(Carbon, Hydrogen, Oxygen)
Plastic figures/blocks	**(Carbon, hydrogen, oxygen, nitrogen, sulfur, chlorine, fluorine, phosphorous, and silicon)**

YIELD: An understanding of chemical elements, based on common household items

TIPS AND HINTS

God's creation brims with wonder! Sadly, we often ignore common things. Uncovering the basic elements of the universe in your home is just one way to help children discover His world. Make time to look carefully with your children at the most "mundane." Ask lots of open-ended and probing questions. Use the Five Common Topics as a resource, and you'll soon find that the ordinary becomes an opportunity for revealing the glory of God.

MICROSCOPE AND TELESCOPE CHART

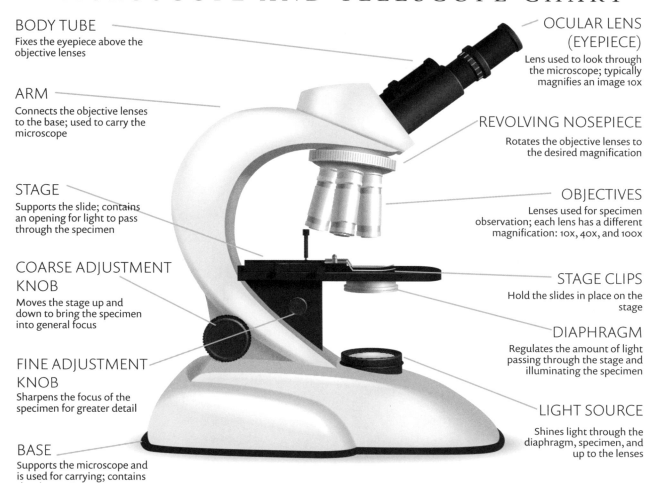

BODY TUBE
Fixes the eyepiece above the objective lenses

ARM
Connects the objective lenses to the base; used to carry the microscope

STAGE
Supports the slide; contains an opening for light to pass through the specimen

COARSE ADJUSTMENT KNOB
Moves the stage up and down to bring the specimen into general focus

FINE ADJUSTMENT KNOB
Sharpens the focus of the specimen for greater detail

BASE
Supports the microscope and is used for carrying; contains the electronics

OCULAR LENS (EYEPIECE)
Lens used to look through the microscope; typically magnifies an image 10x

REVOLVING NOSEPIECE
Rotates the objective lenses to the desired magnification

OBJECTIVES
Lenses used for specimen observation; each lens has a different magnification: 10x, 40x, and 100x

STAGE CLIPS
Hold the slides in place on the stage

DIAPHRAGM
Regulates the amount of light passing through the stage and illuminating the specimen

LIGHT SOURCE
Shines light through the diaphragm, specimen, and up to the lenses

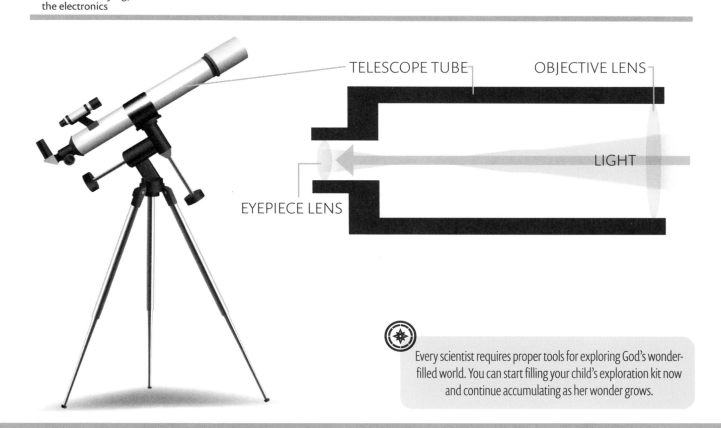

TELESCOPE TUBE

OBJECTIVE LENS

LIGHT

EYEPIECE LENS

Every scientist requires proper tools for exploring God's wonder-filled world. You can start filling your child's exploration kit now and continue accumulating as her wonder grows.

SERVING SUGGESTION: Kitchen

PREP TIME: 45 minutes

INGREDIENTS: Butter (softened), sugar, eggs, flour, baking powder, milk, vanilla extract, (enough ingredients for two cakes), four cake pans or two 9" x 12" pans, paper, pencil, measuring cups, bowls, mixer, spoons, spray oil

STEPS: It's time to bake!

1. Gather your family and divide them into two teams. Supply each team with the listed ingredients and supplies.
2. Without looking, have them choose either Recipe 1 or Recipe 2.
3. Remind them that they must follow the recipe exactly and cannot consult the other team or a cookbook.
4. Enjoy your baked creations together and discuss the results.
5. Award a prize to the team with the best cake or the best team spirit!

Recipe 1: Basic White Cake
Serving Suggestion: Dessert for dinner
Prep Time: 1 hour, including baking and cooling time
Ingredients:

- ☐ 1 cup butter, softened
- ☐ 2 cups sugar
- ☐ 4 large eggs
- ☐ 3 cups flour
- ☐ 1 tablespoon baking powder
- ☐ 1 cup milk
- ☐ 2 teaspoons vanilla extract

Instructions:

1. Preheat oven to 350°. Grease and flour 2 (9-inch) round cake pans. (You can use baking spray with flour.)
2. In a large bowl, beat butter and sugar with a mixer at medium speed until fluffy, 3 to 4 minutes. Add eggs, one at a time, beating well after each addition.
3. In a medium bowl, stir together dry ingredients. Gradually add flour mixture to butter mixture alternately with milk, beginning and ending with flour mixture, beating just until combined after each addition. Stir in vanilla.
4. Pour batter into prepared pans (smoothing tops if necessary). Bake until a wooden pick inserted in center comes out clean, 28 to 30 minutes. Let cool in pans for 10 minutes. Remove from pans and let cool completely on wire racks.

Yield: 2-layer cake

Recipe 2: Basic White Cake
Serving Suggestion: Dessert for dinner
Prep Time: A while
Ingredients:

- ☐ Some sticks of butter
- ☐ Scoops of sugar
- ☐ A few eggs
- ☐ Lots of flour
- ☐ A smidgen of baking powder
- ☐ Milk
- ☐ A few spoons of vanilla extract

Instructions:

1. Turn on the oven and grease your pans.
2. Mix things all together until it looks about right.
3. Pour the batter into a pan and cook for a while.

Yield: _____

YIELD: Lots of laughs as you discover the need for accuracy and clarity

TIPS AND HINTS

To gently introduce precise writing skills to your at-home learners, encourage them to use accurate language in explaining a concept or in the retelling of a story. Mildly guide them to add details and more precise language to clarify their ideas. Sequencing activities also build skills for precision in communicating. Mostly, have a good laugh when confusion ensues and cakes turn out wacky!

LAB REPORT CHART

For decades, the standard practice for scientists to document their experiments has been achieved through the writing of laboratory reports. While there is no standard format for lab reports, this version shows the typical sections, voice, and style.

Title	Name of experiment	**Experiment 1: Diffusion**
Purpose	What the experiment will attempt to demonstrate	The purpose of this experiment is to investigate the process of diffusion between a cornstarch and water mixture and a water and iodine solution, using a baggie as a membrane.
Background	Review of existing knowledge; background information	Diffusion is the random motion of molecules from an area of higher concentration to an area of lower concentration. Diffusion differs from osmosis in that osmosis occurs in water while diffusion can occur in air.
Experimental Procedure	List of all equipment and materials used in the experiment Detailed description of the methods used to conduct the experiment	Equipment and materials used in the experiment were as follows: plastic bag (1) water (125 mL) beaker (250 mL) cornstarch (6 g) iodine (ten drops) eyedropper (1) A plastic baggie was filled with 125 mL of water and 6 grams of cornstarch. A 250 mL beaker was filled with 125 mL of tap water to which ten drops of iodine were added. The baggie was placed in the beaker so that the cornstarch mixture was submerged in the iodine-water solution. An interval of 15 minutes elapsed and then the results were observed.
Results	Final outcome Chart, graph, table, etc. of the experimental raw data	The solution in the bag turned color, going from white to purple. The solution in the beaker did not change color. Table 1. Observable reactions in each solution.

	Initial color	Final color
Solution in beaker	orange	orange
Solution in bag	white	purple

Discussion	Analysis of the results	The solution in the beaker did not change color, while the solution in the baggie changed color from white to purple. The results suggest that the iodine moved into the bag, indicating that it is a permeable membrane. The starch did not move, suggesting that the baggie is a selectively permeable membrane.
Conclusion	Whether the experiment was conclusive or inconclusive	The results of this experiment conclusively demonstrated the principle of diffusion. Iodine moved from an area of higher concentration (beaker) to an area of lower concentration (bag). The starch in the solution did not move, indicating that the baggie served as a semipermeable membrane. Iodine acted as an indicator in this experiment because it turned color in the presence of starch.
References	Sources used to conduct experiment and write lab report	Mays, John D. *The Student Lab Report Handbook.* Novare Science and Math, 2009. Print. Wile, Jay L. *Exploring Creation through Biology, 2nd Edition.* Apologia Educational Ministries, Inc., 2005. Print.

Classical Conversations students work on producing formal lab reports in the Challenge program.

GRAMMAR OF
HISTORY

CHURCH HISTORY TIMELINE CHART

AD 0–100

Pentecost

Acts of the Apostles

Missionary Journeys

Persecution of Christians

Titus and Fall of Jerusalem

100–300s

Apologists and Martyrs

Desert Fathers

Constantine the Great

First Council of Nicea

Augustine of Hippo

Jerome Completes the Vulgate

400–600s

Visigoths Sack Rome

Council of Chalcedon

Fall of Western Roman Empire

Justinian and Theodora

Benedict and Monasticism

Rise of Islam

700–1100s

Iconoclast Controversy

Charlemagne

Vladimir and Russian Orthodoxy

Popes and Patriarchs

East-West Schism

1100–1500s

The Crusades

Avignon Papacy

Gutenberg's Printing Press

Conciliar Movement

Fall of Constantinople

1500–1600s

Inquisition

Protestant Reformation

Council of Trent

Patriarchate of Moscow

1700–1800s

First and Second Great Awakenings

Global Missions

First Vatican Council

African Methodist Episcopal Church

Rise of Startsy in Russia

20TH CENTURY

Fundamentalism and Pentecostalism

Persecution of Jews and Christians

World Council of Churches

Second Vatican Council

Growth of Chinese Church

Start with this timeline and add other events as you go. Fixing some dates and happenings in our minds brings context and understanding as we continue to learn about people, places, conflicts, and discoveries.

HISTORY

SERVING SUGGESTION: In the car

PREP TIME: 10 minutes

INGREDIENTS: *Foundations Memory Work Flashcards*, or a personally selected history sentence about a president or world leader. The sentence should include a date, a person, a place, and an event. Here is an example: "In 1789, in New York, George Washington was granted the full powers and responsibilities of the presidency by the U.S. Constitution" (*Foundations Curriculum*, Cycle 3 Week 5 History).

STEPS:
1. Write out the memory sentence that you have chosen on an index card or grab the *Memory Work Flashcards*.
2. As you head out the door, bring it along.
3. While you're waiting at a traffic light or in a drive-through, have everyone practice saying the memory sentence.
4. Repeat it several times aloud. As you go, pause before the next part and have your child fill it in. Emphasize the different parts with your voice. Say it in a silly voice or with an accent. Say it in a yell. Say it in a whisper. Say it slowly. Say it quickly.

YIELD: A child who is building a storehouse of historical knowledge one peg at a time

TIPS AND HINTS

Have you been surprised by the catchy songs or rhymes that your young children can recite? It's surprising how easily young children can memorize facts, rhymes, poems, songs, and even cereal jingles! To take advantage of this season, fill your child's mind with information that builds an internal library. Fill those shelves with relevant and edifying facts about our natural world, history, language, literature, and math. Leigh Bortins writes in *The Core*: "To build the brain's knowledge store, you begin by memorizing orderly systems. You do that by visiting the 'store of words' for any particular subject many times in an organized manner. For a student, it means repeating data (revisiting the store in an orderly fashion)—filling the shelves" (51).

UNITED STATES PRESIDENTS CHART

Washington	Adams	Jefferson	Madison	Monroe	Adams	Jackson
Van Buren	Harrison	Tyler	Polk	Taylor	Fillmore	Pierce
Buchanan	Lincoln	Johnson	Grant	Hayes	Garfield	Arthur
Cleveland	Harrison	Cleveland	McKinley	Roosevelt	Taft	Wilson
Harding	Coolidge	Hoover	Roosevelt	Truman	Eisenhower	Kennedy
Johnson	Nixon	Ford	Carter	Reagan	Bush	Clinton

Bush   Obama   Trump   Biden

Students in the Foundations program will work on memorizing the U.S. presidents; U.S. Challenge students will flesh out their study of these leaders as they focus on documents, history, and leadership themes in other strands.

HISTORY

SERVING SUGGESTION: Living room floor

PREP TIME: 15 minutes

INGREDIENTS: Map of your country, reference source, markers, paper, or large sticky notes

STEPS:
1. Find a picture of your country's flag.
2. Look at it carefully and discover a few facts from your reference source that explain the colors and symbols.
3. Discuss with one another other symbols that represent your country.
4. Draw one symbol and a picture of the flag.
5. Place them on your map. As an extension, consider: Do you have family members or friends who live in other countries? Look up their flags and tape them to your map.
6. Celebrate the beauty of God's people in His world.

YIELD: A child who is learning about what makes the history and peoples of the world's countries special

TIPS AND HINTS

Nations are shaped by boundaries. Boundaries can change; however, a country's fundamental identity doesn't. A nation's symbols represent its values, traditions, history, and beliefs. The study of flags and symbols helps us gain a better understanding of our neighbors. As children's vision of the world is expanded through the study of geography, students "learn and discuss a sweeping, yet detailed, study of world history" *Challenge IV Guide* (22).

FORMS OF GOVERNMENT CHART

WHO RULES?

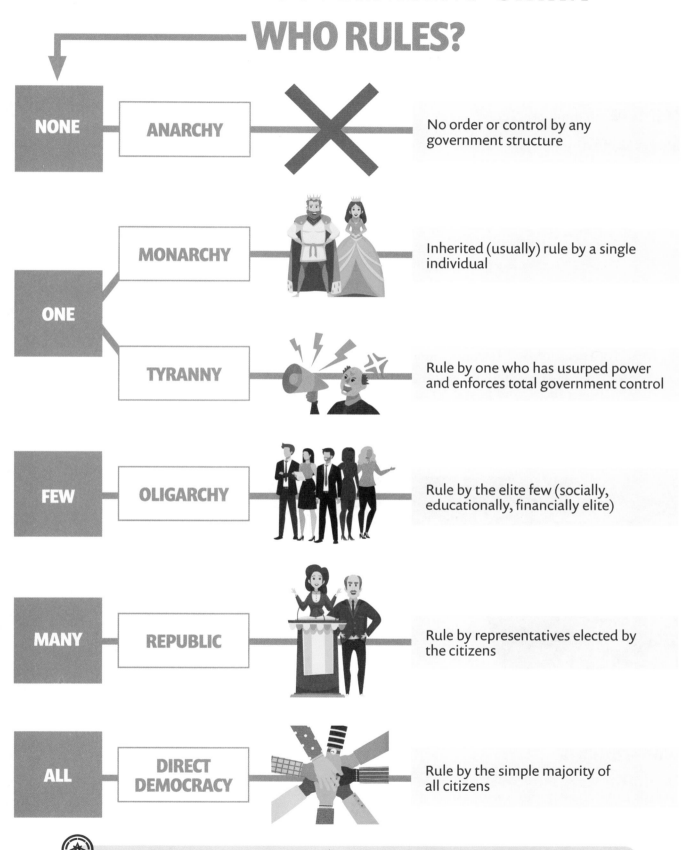

NONE — **ANARCHY** — No order or control by any government structure

ONE — **MONARCHY** — Inherited (usually) rule by a single individual

ONE — **TYRANNY** — Rule by one who has usurped power and enforces total government control

FEW — **OLIGARCHY** — Rule by the elite few (socially, educationally, financially elite)

MANY — **REPUBLIC** — Rule by representatives elected by the citizens

ALL — **DIRECT DEMOCRACY** — Rule by the simple majority of all citizens

Many political and economic systems used throughout the world today fit within these broad categories. Challenge students will wrestle with the ideologies represented as they study history, philosophy, theology, and literature.

PUBLIC SPEAKING CHART

Public speaking is the art of writing aloud.

	Persuasive	Expository	Impromptu	Memorized
Faculty	**Discernment** *appealing to a point of view*	**Interpretation** *assisting understanding*	**Imagination** *recalling from experience*	**Memoria** *reciting from memory*
Definition	To advocate for a particular decision in a community	To suggest a truth discovered by attending to the form and context of a text or texts	To quickly invent and organize thoughts with little to no preparation	To deliver word for word a speech written by someone else
Practice Strand	Exposition/Debate	Exposition/Debate/Research	Debate	Exposition/Debate
Artifact	Debates Campaigns Advertisements	Lectures Sermons Demonstrations	Interviews Testimonies Entertainments	Actors' Lines Poetry Recitations Ceremonial Addresses

TOOLS

Modes of Persuasion

Ethos: *An appeal based on the speaker's character or ethical reputation; speaker gains trust and respect*

Logos: *An appeal to one's reason or understanding; speaker makes logical arguments*

Pathos: *An appeal to one's emotions; speaker generates anger, fear, pity, or love*

The Five Common Topics

Definition *Discover what something is*

Comparison *Discover similarities first, then differences*

Relationship *Discover causes and effects*

Circumstance *Discover what else is happening at the same time in other places*

Testimony/Authority *Discover what others say*

The Five Canons of Rhetoric

Invention *Thinking of what to say*

Arrangement *Arranging ideas in logical; organized manner*

Elocution *Expressing ideas in a style that appeals to audience*

Memory *Adding memorable features to the speech*

Delivery *Delivering ideas orally*

Rhetoric
Memory
Intensity, Duration, Repetition

Delivery
Eye contact, posture, movement, gesture, energy, facial expression, volume, enunciation, pacing, tone

Throughout the Classical Conversations Challenge program, students focus on persuasive oral communication—public speaking! They learn the rules and nuances of formal debate, construct grant presentations, work on dramatic speeches, and practice leading discussions.

SERVING SUGGESTION: On the living room floor or on the bed

PREP TIME: 5 minutes to gather "characters"

INGREDIENTS: Seven stuffed animals, action figures, or plastic animals; script (below)

STEPS:
1. Choose stuffed animals to represent Goldilocks, Papa Bear, Mama Bear, Baby Bear, Lead Prosecuting Attorney, Judge, and Defense Attorney.
2. Read the opening statement aloud.
3. Have each child place each "character" in the correct part of the courtroom.
4. As each character is mentioned, have the child introduce herself as the character or repeat parts of the statements. (Older children may wish to continue the trial following the order of the trial listed at right.)

Mock Trial Sample Opening Statement: The Case against Goldilocks

Your honor, my name is _____, and as the prosecuting attorney, I shall be making the opening remarks in this case. Allow me to introduce plaintiffs Papa Bear, Mama Bear, and Baby Bear.

This case is about a juvenile delinquent who not only broke into a house, but also shattered the sense of security for a family, forever. On the peaceful morning of April 1, 2019, Papa Bear and his family were having a breakfast of porridge. However, because Papa Bear's porridge was too hot, and Mama Bear's was too cold, the Bear family went for a walk in the woods. Believing that their neighborhood was safe, they left their door unlocked.

The defendant, Goldilocks, broke into the Bear household. First, she went through their porridge, eating all of Baby Bear's porridge. She then broke Baby Bear's chair. Goldilocks then decided to go into the bedroom and mess up all of their bedspreads. The defendant then slept in Baby Bear's bed.

The plaintiffs, the Bear family, returned from their walk about an hour later. They went into their dining room and found that someone had been eating their food. Baby Bear found his chair broken. Then, Papa Bear and Mama Bear went into their bedroom and found that someone had been sleeping in their bed. And they found Goldilocks still sleeping in Baby Bear's bed. Goldilocks woke up and ran off before the police could be called.

We will prove that Goldilocks committed a trespass because she entered the Bear household without permission. We will also prove that she committed property damage by eating Baby Bear's food and destroying his chair.

Our first witness will be Papa Bear. Papa Bear is a hardworking bear, who has narrowly avoided being captured and put in a zoo. Tired of dodging tranquilizer darts, he moved into this neighborhood to start a new life and a new family. However, Papa Bear found out that he still had to live in fear. He will testify that it was Goldilocks who broke into his house on April 1, 2019. Papa Bear got a good, long look at the defendant as she lay sleeping in Baby Bear's bed. It was Papa Bear who picked out Goldilocks in the lineup at the police station.

Our second witness will be Mama Bear. Mama Bear decided to give up a career performing in the circus in order to care for her young son. Mama Bear will testify about how she bought and cooked porridge on April 1, 2019. Mama Bear will explain how she picked out a chair for Baby Bear and how the chair was "just right." She will also testify about how she no longer wants the family to leave the house for walks.

Our final witness will be Baby Bear. Baby Bear will tell this court how hungry he was because his porridge had been eaten. Baby Bear will also testify that since the break in, he has nightmares and cannot sleep in his own bed because he is afraid.

We are asking that the court find Goldilocks liable for property damage and infliction of emotional distress and award monetary damages to the Bears. On April 1, 2019, Goldilocks did not just break into the Bears' house, she did not just eat the Bears' food, she did not just vandalize the Bears' furniture, she shattered their sense of security.

YIELD: Children with the beginnings of understanding of the trial process

TIPS AND HINTS

From Foundations to Challenge, students are given opportunities each week to stand in front of a loving group of people and present. It starts small—a brief show-and-tell moment—and ends with long, memorized historical speeches, two-hour team policy debates, recitations from great dramas, and cross-examinations at a Mock Trial event. That's how most home education works. We start with small, seemingly insignificant events, and as they are cultivated over time, these events become opportunities for clear articulation and moving presentations. Students learn that truth can be spoken in ways that are beautiful and winsome.

MOCK TRIAL CHART

ORDER OF THE TRIAL

Each trial will consist of two rounds.

Each team is required to present both a prosecution case and a defense case.

I. COIN TOSS – Before Round 1

II. OPENING THE COURT – Bailiff will open court

III. OPENING REMARKS – Judge's opening remarks

IV. PLEA – Judge will ask defendant to enter plea

V. PRE-TRIAL MOTIONS – As a standard procedure, the judge will ask for any pre-trial motions; however, NO PRE-TRIAL MOTIONS are permitted in Mock Trial.

VI. OPENING STATEMENTS
Prosecution Opening Statement
Defense Opening Statement

VII. PROSECUTION'S CASE
1st Prosecution Witness – Direct examination
    Defense – Cross-examination
2nd Prosecution Witness – Direct examination
    Defense – Cross-examination

VIII. DEFENSE'S CASE
1st Defense Witness – Direct examination
    Prosecution – Cross-examination
2nd Defense Witness – Direct examination
    Prosecution – Cross-examination
3rd Defense Witness – Direct examination
    Prosecution – Cross-examination

IX. CLOSING ARGUMENTS
Defense Closing Argument
Prosecution Closing Argument

X. RECESS – Intertrial Recess
(After recess, repeat trial order for second round.)

 Mock Trial is the signature event of Challenge B; it calls upon the students to use their logic skills along with persuasive writing and speaking skills. Students learn to appreciate and use the formal structure of the trial to tell a compelling story of what happened in a dispute. They also learn to value the freedoms this structure promotes and protects.

SERVING SUGGESTION: In the living room

PREP TIME: 3 minutes per child

INGREDIENTS: Index cards and pencils

STEPS:
1. Before you head out to the grocery store, gather your children. Ask them to consider which cereal you should purchase at the store.

2. Give each child a 3 × 5 note card or half a sheet of notebook paper.

3. Have them fold their card in half. On one side have them write their name and a brief description of their position.

   For example: "Hello, my name is Jan. I am presenting my reasons that Cheerios should be our cereal of choice."

4. On the other side, have them write (or dictate) three reasons for purchasing their favorite cereal.

5. Before the cereal debate begins, review the rules of good listening and polite responses if your choice is not supported.

6. Start the cereal debate. Have each child present his or her case and end the presentation with, "I now stand ready for questions."

7. Give everyone a few minutes to ask questions before the next child's presentation.

8. As the moderator (parent), give brief feedback and what your final decision is.

9. After going to the store, have a cereal celebration! (Maybe purchase each type that was debated and have a taste-testing time.)

YIELD: A child who begins to understand the differences between debating and arguing; a child who recognizes that structured interchanges allow people to respectfully discuss competing ideas

TIPS AND HINTS

It may seem like the last thing you want to do is *encourage* debate in your home. While it's true that debating badly (fighting) is harmful, true debating is actually a way for conflict to bring us closer to discovering truth. Christ spent time on earth challenging ideas with reason and grace. He was measured and thoughtful in His approach to others, even those who were His worst enemies. Consider Christ's response to the Pharisees when they ask Him if they should pay a tax to Caesar. He responds by first confronting them regarding their motive: "Why are you testing Me, you hypocrites?" Then, He asks for evidence of the coin. His question "Whose likeness and inscription is this?" is a measured confrontation. His final words are profound and challenge the motive and beliefs of the Pharisees: "Then render to Caesar the things that are Caesar's and to God the things that are God's." Can you see why the Pharisees left marveling? Trace Jesus' argument—if we render to Caesar what is his because his image is on the coin, then whose image is stamped on us? So, we are left with more than an answer about taxes. Jesus' response penetrates the hypocritical thinking and strikes at our hearts. This is the true purpose of debate.

DEBATE CHART

TEAM POLICY

In **Team Policy debate,** two teams advocate either for or against a resolution that calls for government policy change. A sample resolution might be: *The federal government should adopt a nuclear weapon policy of no first use.*

First Affirmative Constructive
1A stands, introduces self and partner, states resolution, defines terms, presents harms, plan, and advantages.

2N joins the 1A. Cross-examination of 1A by 2N.

First Negative Constructive
1N stands, introduces self and partner, rejects resolution, accepts or rejects AFF's terms, attacks AFF's harms, plan, and advantages.

1A joins the 1N. Cross-examination of 1N by 1A.

Second Affirmative Constructive
2A stands, refutes all of 1N's arguments, rebuilds and strengthens AFF case with new evidence.

1N joins the 2A. Cross-examination of 2A by 1N.

Second Negative Constructive
2N stands, refutes 2A's counter-arguments, elaborates NEG's arguments, presents new evidence.

2A joins the 2N. Cross-examination of 2N by 2A.

First Negative Rebuttal
2A and 2N sit. 1N stands, expands partner's strongest issues. Explains superiority of NEG's arguments.

First Affirmative Rebuttal
1N sits. 1A stands, responds quickly to all NEG arguments, explains superiority of AFF's case, attacks new arguments raised in rebuttal.

Second Negative Rebuttal
1A sits. 2N stands, refutes all arguments of 1AR, defends status quo, explains why NEG should win.

Second Affirmative Rebuttal
2N sits. 2A stands, traces AFF arguments from beginning to end, explains need for change, why AFF should win.

LINCOLN-DOUGLAS

Lincoln-Douglas debate is a one-on-one debate over values (usually moral principles such as liberty, justice, free speech, etc.). A sample resolution might be: *Civil disobedience in a democracy is morally justified.*

Affirmative Constructive
AFF stands, introduces self, states resolution, defines terms, names the value at stake and the criterion for defining and measuring the value, lists contentions (logical proof) with evidence.

NEG joins the AFF. Cross-examination of AFF by NEG.

Negative Constructive
AFF sits. NEG introduces self, rejects resolution, accepts or rejects AFF's terms, accepts value or names alternative, lists contentions with evidence, attacks AFF's contentions.

AFF joins the NEG. Cross-examination of NEG by AFF.

First Affirmative Rebuttal
Synthesizes both sides of the argument, responds quickly to all NEG arguments, explains superiority of AFF value.

Negative Rebuttal
Reviews NEG case, repeats NEG's strongest arguments, explains why NEG's value should prevail.

Second Affirmative Rebuttal
Repeats AFF case, emphasizes why AFF's value is the better value to uphold, and why the AFF should win.

How many OiLS (circles, dots, straight lines, angled lines, curved lines) can you find in this picture? Your children can use pictures like this to grow their attending skills as well as their sketching skills; both skills will pay dividends throughout their years of formal education.

BIBLE

LITERATURE

SERVING SUGGESTION: Church

PREP TIME: 5 seconds

INGREDIENTS: Bible

STEPS:
1. In the Bible's table of contents, quietly point to the name of a book and ask your child to find that title in the body of the Bible.

2. There are many versions of this game, depending on your child's ability. In general, this list goes from easiest to hardest. Ask your child to find:

   - a page number such as 9

   - a page sequence such as 9, 99, 999

   - a book title with the page number on the table of contents (find the page where that book starts); a page with a book title (find the book title and page number on the table of contents)

   - the count of a common word, such as "God" or "love," on a specific page you have already skimmed to be sure the word is on the page multiple times

Not only is your child getting used to managing a large, heavy book with no pictures, your child is also getting practice in one-to-one correspondence, counting, sequencing, and reading. At first it is very difficult and random. Do the task together, silently, while pointing until your child understands what you are doing. He will pay very close attention because you cannot speak.

For example, point to the word "John" in the table of contents, turn to the back of the book and show the usually larger font titles of "John" as well as a few of normal font in the text. Then it's your child's turn to point to a table of contents book, such as "Micah," and you find that title in the body and text. Then go back and forth, choosing which title to find. Eventually, your child will notice how the page numbers in the table of contents help to find a book of the Bible. In some Bibles, the title page in the Bible's body doesn't have a page number, so you will need to show to look at page numbers before or after the one on the table of contents.

YIELD: A quiet child learning the organization of the Bible

TIPS AND HINTS

Around the age of four, most children can match symbols. You can play a variety of silent games with your children that keeps them interested in the Bible while sitting during the pastor's sermon. You want them to learn how to quickly find the sermon when they are older and use their fingers to hold the place of different pages in order to cross reference the ideas in the Bible. It is difficult to train your children to attend. Thankfully, church provides an opportunity to teach children to think quietly and exercise self-control for a set time each week during the sermon. We adults have to believe it is possible before we will believe it is worthwhile.

BIBLE GENRES CHART

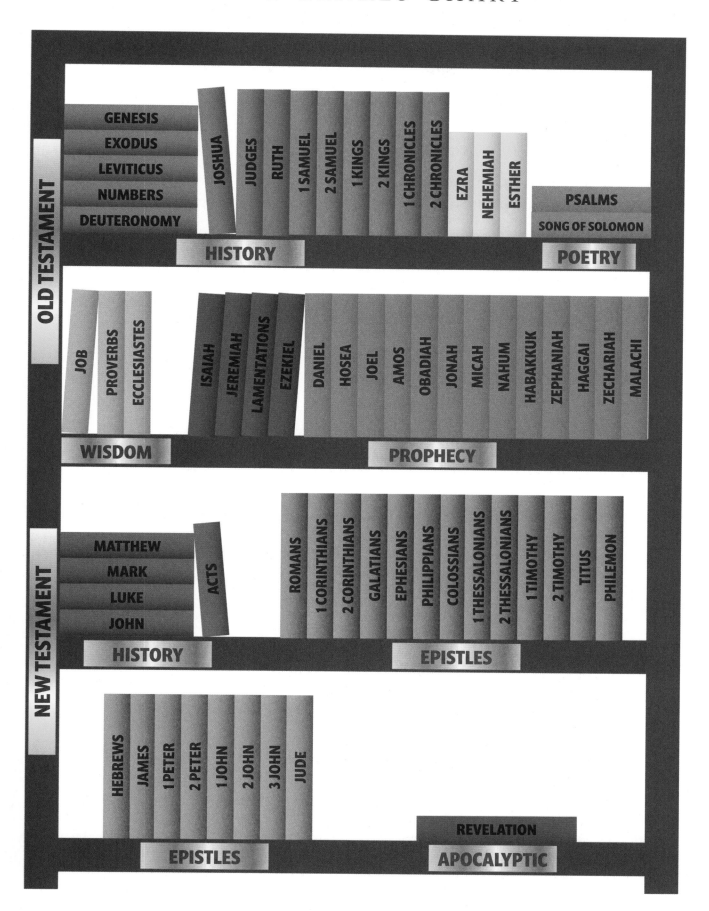

OLD TESTAMENT

GENESIS
EXODUS
LEVITICUS
NUMBERS
DEUTERONOMY
JOSHUA
JUDGES
RUTH
1 SAMUEL
2 SAMUEL
1 KINGS
2 KINGS
1 CHRONICLES
2 CHRONICLES
EZRA
NEHEMIAH
ESTHER

HISTORY

PSALMS
SONG OF SOLOMON

POETRY

JOB
PROVERBS
ECCLESIASTES

WISDOM

ISAIAH
JEREMIAH
LAMENTATIONS
EZEKIEL
DANIEL
HOSEA
JOEL
AMOS
OBADIAH
JONAH
MICAH
NAHUM
HABAKKUK
ZEPHANIAH
HAGGAI
ZECHARIAH
MALACHI

PROPHECY

NEW TESTAMENT

MATTHEW
MARK
LUKE
JOHN
ACTS

HISTORY

ROMANS
1 CORINTHIANS
2 CORINTHIANS
GALATIANS
EPHESIANS
PHILIPPIANS
COLOSSIANS
1 THESSALONIANS
2 THESSALONIANS
1 TIMOTHY
2 TIMOTHY
TITUS
PHILEMON

EPISTLES

HEBREWS
JAMES
1 PETER
2 PETER
1 JOHN
2 JOHN
3 JOHN
JUDE

EPISTLES

REVELATION

APOCALYPTIC

SERVING SUGGESTION: Couch and coffee table, yard and picnic table, or porch and floor

PREP TIME: 5 minutes to gather drawing supplies

INGREDIENTS: Bible, Temple Pillars Chart (at right), drawing supplies

STEPS:
1. Read 1 Kings 7:15–22 aloud with your family.

2. Read this descriptive Bible passage aloud again, sentence by sentence, and try to draw what you hear. Lots of description and discussion may take place before any circles, straight lines, dots, angled lines, or curved lines are drawn. (Think of this as another way to remember Bible stories: Noah's ark, the temple ark, the manger scene, stars and angels, and more!)

3. Try narrating, discussing, and drawing this mathematical passage with older children. Just discuss a few features the first time, and then discuss a few more the next time you do this activity. Let younger children trace and color the pillars (on the accompanying chart) as you read each sentence from 1 Kings 7:15 and following (NIV).

    He cast (What is *casting*?)

    two (How many?)

    bronze (What material?)

    pillars, (What is a *pillar*?)

    each eighteen cubits high (What is a *cubit*?)

    and twelve cubits in circumference. (What is *circumference*?)

    He also made two capitals of cast bronze . . . (What is a *capital*?)

    A network of interwoven chains adorned the capitals . . . (What is *interwoven*?)

    He made pomegranates in two rows encircling each network . . . (What is a *pomegranate*?)

    The capitals on top of the pillars in the portico were in the shape of lilies, four cubits high . . . (What is a *lily*?)

    The pillar to the south he named Jakin and the one to the north Boaz. (What would you have called the pillars?)

YIELD: Children who happily imitate their Creator by ably drawing what they see or hear described; a family who reads Scripture together

TIPS AND HINTS

Children like to draw. They tend to draw with great confidence until they are about eight years old. Then they become aware that they don't draw as accurately as they would like to and their enthusiasm can dwindle. Teaching them to attend to their surroundings and using the OiLS technique to draw can guide them through any confidence barriers.

Have your child narrate his drawing to you, describing what he is drawing either as he draws or after the drawing is complete.

Narration can be used to practice drawing as a family; this is also a lovely, restful way to attend to God's Word together.

WEEK 9

- ☐ Mephibosheth: 2 Samuel 4:4; 9:1–13
- ☐ David's Sin: 2 Samuel 11:1–12:25
- ☐ Solomon Becomes King: 1 Kings 2:1–12
- ☐ God's Gift to Solomon: 1 Kings 3:16–28

WEEK 10

- ☐ Solomon Builds the Temple: 1 Kings 6
- ☐ Queen of Sheba: 1 Kings 10:1–13
- ☐ Solomon Dies: 1 Kings 11
- ☐ Israel Divides into Two Kingdoms: 2 Chronicles 10

WEEK 11

- ☐ King Nadab: 1 Kings 15:25–32
- ☐ King Baasha: 1 Kings 15:27–16:7
- ☐ King Zimri: 1 Kings 16:15–20
- ☐ King Omri: 1 Kings 16:21–28

WEEK 12

- ☐ Israel Falls to Assyria: 2 Kings 17
- ☐ Elijah and the Ravens: 1 Kings 16:29–17:9
- ☐ Elijah and the Widow: 1 Kings 17: 10–24
- ☐ Elijah in Hiding: 1 Kings 18:1–16

WEEK 13

- ☐ Elijah and the Prophets of Baal: 1 Kings 18:17–46
- ☐ Elijah in the Cave: 1 Kings 19
- ☐ Ahab and Syria: 1 Kings 20
- ☐ Naboth's Vineyard: 1 Kings 21

WEEK 14

- ☐ Elijah and the Chariot of Fire: 2 Kings 2
- ☐ Elisha and the Miracle of Oil: 2 Kings 4:1–7
- ☐ Elisha and the Miracle of the Boy: 2 Kings 4:8–36
- ☐ Elisha and the Miracle of Naaman: 2 Kings 5:1–14

WEEK 15

- ☐ Elisha's Servant: 2 Kings 5:15–27
- ☐ God Protects Elisha: 2 Kings 6:8–23
- ☐ Jonah Runs from God: Jonah 1
- ☐ Jonah in the Whale: Jonah 2

WEEK 16

- ☐ Jonah Goes to Nineveh: Jonah 3
- ☐ Jonah and the Vine: Jonah 4
- ☐ King Rehoboam: 1 Kings 12:1–24
- ☐ King Jehoshaphat: 1 Kings 22:41–50

WEEK 17

- ☐ Joash, the Boy King: 2 Chronicles 22:11–23
- ☐ Joash Repairs the Temple: 2 Chronicles 24
- ☐ King Hezekiah Threatened by Sennacherib: 2 Kings 18:1–16; 26–37
- ☐ King Hezekiah's Prayer: 2 Kings 19:14–37

WEEK 18

- ☐ King Hezekiah's Illness: 2 Kings 20:1–11
- ☐ King Josiah and the Finding of the Law: 2 Kings 22
- ☐ King Josiah Renews the Covenant: 2 Kings 23:1–15
- ☐ King Josiah Purges the Land: 2 Kings 23:16–30

WEEK 19

- ☐ Isaiah Sees God: Isaiah 6:1–8
- ☐ Isaiah Prophesies about Jesus: Isaiah 7:10–17
- ☐ Isaiah's Message of Comfort: Isaiah 40:1–11
- ☐ Jeremiah and the Potter's House: Jeremiah 18

WEEK 20

- ☐ Judah Falls to Babylon: 2 Chronicles 36:15–23
- ☐ Ezekiel and the Chariot: Ezekiel 1
- ☐ Ezekiel and the Dry Bones: Ezekiel 37:1–14
- ☐ Daniel and His Friends: Daniel 1

WEEK 21

- ☐ The Fiery Furnace: Daniel 3
- ☐ The Writing on the Wall: Daniel 5
- ☐ Daniel in the Lion's Den: Daniel 6
- ☐ Homecoming: Ezra 1

WEEK 22

- ☐ Rebuilding the Altar and Temple: Ezra 3
- ☐ Trouble Rebuilding: Ezra 4
- ☐ Temple Rebuilt: Ezra 6
- ☐ Return to Jerusalem: Ezra 8:15–36

WEEK 23

- ☐ Esther Becomes Queen: Esther 2:1–18
- ☐ Haman Plots to Kill the Jews: Esther 3
- ☐ Esther's Petitions to the King: Esther 5:1–8, Esther 7
- ☐ Nehemiah's Prayer: Nehemiah 1

WEEK 24

- ☐ Nehemiah in Jerusalem: Nehemiah 2
- ☐ Rebuilding the Walls: Nehemiah 3
- ☐ Finishing the Walls: Nehemiah 6:15–7:3
- ☐ Ezra Reads the Law: Nehemiah 8:1–12

BIBLE

CYCLE THREE

WEEK 1
- ☐ Angel Visits Zacharias: Luke 1:1–23
- ☐ Angel Visits Mary: Luke 1:24–56
- ☐ Baby John: Luke 1:57–80
- ☐ Jesus' Birth: Luke 2:1–39

WEEK 2
- ☐ The Wise Men: Matthew 2
- ☐ Jesus in the Temple: Luke 2:40–52
- ☐ John the Baptist: Luke 3:1–20
- ☐ Jesus' Baptism and Temptation: Luke 3:21–22; Luke 4:1–14

WEEK 3
- ☐ Jesus Calls Five Disciples: John 1:35–51
- ☐ Wedding at Cana and Passover: John 2
- ☐ Nicodemus: John 3:1–21
- ☐ Woman at the Well: John 4:1–43

WEEK 4
- ☐ Nobleman's Son: John 4:44–54
- ☐ Jesus Speaks at Nazareth: Luke 4:16–32
- ☐ Jesus Calls Peter, Andrew, James & John: Luke 5:1–11; Mark 1:16–38
- ☐ Jesus Calls Matthew: Matthew 9:9–13

WEEK 5
- ☐ Healings: John 5:1–18; Luke 6:1–11
- ☐ Sermon on the Mount: Matthew 5
- ☐ Sermon on the Mount: Matthew 6
- ☐ Sermon on the Mount: Matthew 7

WEEK 6
- ☐ Leper and Centurion: Matthew 8:1–13
- ☐ The Paralytic: Luke 5:18–26
- ☐ Widow's Son and John the Baptist in Prison: Luke 7:11–23
- ☐ Woman Anoints Jesus' Feet: Luke 7:36–50

WEEK 7
- ☐ Parable of the Sower: Mark 4:1–20
- ☐ Jesus Calms the Storm: Mark 4:21–41
- ☐ Jesus Casts Out Demons: Luke 5:1–20
- ☐ Other Miracles: Mark 5:22–43

WEEK 8
- ☐ Five Loaves and Two Fish: Mark 6:30–46
- ☐ Jesus Walks on Water: Mark 6:47–56
- ☐ Gentile Woman and Feeding of 5,000: Mark 7:24–8:10
- ☐ Blind Man and Peter's Confession: Mark 8:22–9:1

"The Story of Redeeming Love." Illustration by unknown artist in *The Pictorial Tract Primer* by Frances Manwaring Caulkins (New York: American Tract Society, c. 1850).

WEEK 9

- [ ] Transfiguration: Matthew 17:1–13
- [ ] Who Is the Greatest? Matthew 17:22–18:14
- [ ] A Lesson in Forgiveness: Matthew 18:21–35
- [ ] Jesus and the Children: Matthew 19

WEEK 10

- [ ] The Ten Lepers: Luke 17:11–19
- [ ] The Feast in Jerusalem: John 7:2–53
- [ ] The Pharisees and the Sinful Woman: John 8
- [ ] Jesus Heals the Blind Man: John 9

WEEK 11

- [ ] Good Samaritan: Luke 10:25–37
- [ ] Lazarus Raised from the Dead: John 11:1–54
- [ ] The Prodigal Son: Luke 15:11–32
- [ ] Judge and Publican: Luke 18:1–14

WEEK 12

- [ ] Bartimaeus and Zacchaeus: Luke 18:35–19:10
- [ ] Parable of the Talents: Luke 19:11–27
- [ ] Jesus Rides into Jerusalem as King: Luke 19:29–40
- [ ] Jesus Teaches in the Temple: Luke 19:41–20:17

WEEK 13

- [ ] The Pharisees: Matthew 22:15–23:39
- [ ] Jesus in the Temple: John 12:20–36
- [ ] Parable of Ten Virgins: Matthew 25:1–13
- [ ] The Last Supper: Mark 14:12–26

WEEK 14

- [ ] Jesus Prays in the Garden: Luke 22:39–53
- [ ] Jesus' Arrest and Trials: Luke 22:66–23:25
- [ ] Jesus' Crucifixion: Luke 23:26–56
- [ ] Watchers at the Tomb: Matthew 27:55–28:1

WEEK 15

- [ ] Jesus' Resurrection: Luke 24:1–12
- [ ] Road to Emmaus: Luke 24:13–35
- [ ] Doubting Thomas: John 20:19–31
- [ ] Jesus' Last Meeting with Disciples: Acts 1:1–14

WEEK 16

- [ ] Pentecost: Acts 2:1–21
- [ ] Pentecost: Acts 2:22–47
- [ ] Lame Man at the Gate Beautiful: Acts 3
- [ ] Peter and John in Prison: Acts 4:1–31

WEEK 17

- [ ] The Early Church: Acts 4:32–5:11
- [ ] Angel Opens Prison Doors: Acts 5:12–42
- [ ] Stephen's Arrest: Acts 6:8–15
- [ ] Stephen's Death: Acts 7:54–60

WEEK 18

- [ ] Simon Tries to Buy the Holy Spirit: Acts 8:4–25
- [ ] Philip and the Ethiopian: Acts 8:26–40
- [ ] Road to Damascus: Acts 9:1–8
- [ ] Saul Believes: Acts 9:9–19

WEEK 19

- [ ] Saul's Escape in a Basket: Acts 9:20–31
- [ ] Miracles: Acts 9:32–43
- [ ] Peter and Cornelius: Acts 10:1–11:18
- [ ] Angel Frees Peter: Acts 12:1–23

WEEK 20

- [ ] Barnabas and Saul at Antioch: Acts 11:19–30; 12:24–25
- [ ] Barnabas and Saul as Missionaries: Acts 13:1–13
- [ ] Paul and Barnabas at Antioch and Iconium: Acts 13:14–14:7
- [ ] Paul and Barnabas Mistaken for Gods: Acts 14:8–28

WEEK 21

- [ ] Division in the Church: Acts 15:1–34
- [ ] Paul's Second Journey: Acts 15:36–16:15
- [ ] The Philippian Jailer: Acts 16:16–40
- [ ] Macedonia: Acts 17:1–15

WEEK 22

- [ ] Mars Hill: Acts 17:16–34
- [ ] Corinth: Acts 18:1–23
- [ ] Ephesus: Acts 18:2–19:20
- [ ] Paul Travels to Jerusalem: Acts 20:5–21:17

WEEK 23

- [ ] Paul Taken Prisoner: Acts 21:18–23:10
- [ ] Youth Saves Paul: Acts 23:11–35
- [ ] Paul before Felix: Acts 24:1–26
- [ ] Paul Appeals to Caesar: Acts 24:27–25:12

WEEK 24

- [ ] King Agrippa and Paul: Acts 25:13–26:32
- [ ] Paul's Shipwreck: Acts 27
- [ ] Safety and Arrival in Rome: Acts 28
- [ ] Onesimus: Philemon

APPENDICES

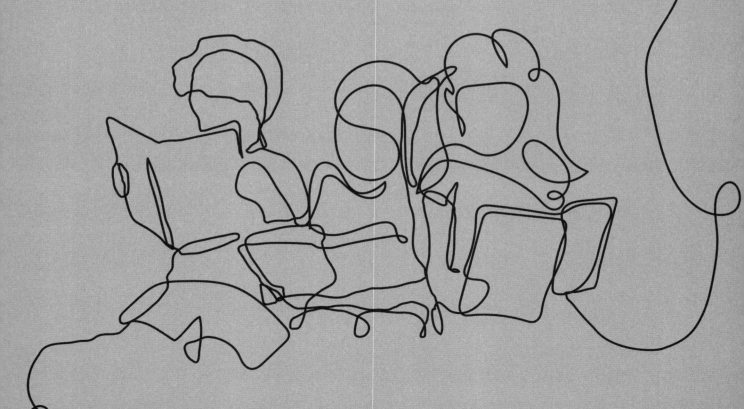

These "staples" will help you cook whatever feels right each day; they provide good ingredients to use as you complete your daily menu! You'll find resources for handwriting, reading and phonics, history, science, and literature for your family to enjoy.

PreScripts® Cursive Words and Drawing: Scripture

PreScripts® Cursive Letters and Coloring: World History

PreScripts® Cursive Words and Drawing: Math Terms

The Writing Road to Reading

Kings of Rome

Senators of Rome

Emperors of Rome

Exploring Insects with Uncle Paul

Exploring the Heavens with Uncle Paul

Exploring the Oceans with Uncle Paul

Ancient World Echoes

Old World Echoes

New World Echoes

Classical Acts & Facts® History Cards:
Ancient World, Medieval World, New World, Modern World

Classical Acts & Facts® Artists and Composers Cards

Classical Acts & Facts® Science Cards

Nature Sketch Journal

Math Flashcards

Quick Flip Arithmetic

Trivium at the Table Maps

Exploring the World Through Cartography

STOCK THE PANTRY